For Sarah, Billy and Jemima

A New Cottage Garden

A practical guide
to creating a
picture-perfect
cottage garden

Mark Bolton

Frontispiece Sunflowers in early autumn at Bowhay House

Right *Allium* 'Purple Sensation' stands high above sweet williams in early summer at Bowhay House

Pimpernel Press Limited
www.pimpernelpress.com

© Pimpernel Press Limited 2024

A NEW COTTAGE GARDEN:
A practical guide to creating a
picture–perfect cottage garden

Text © Mark Bolton 2024
Photographs © Mark Bolton 2024

A catalogue record for this book is available from the British Library.

ISBN 978-1-914902-9-63

Typeset in Lora Regular

Printed and bound in China
by C&C Offset Printing Company Limited

9 8 7 6 5 4 3 2 1

Contents

Foreword

'Among the things made by man, nothing is prettier than an English cottage garden.'
William Robinson

Starting a garden from scratch is one of the most exciting and rewarding things any of us can do. It takes time and work, care and patience, but the rewards of these efforts are infinite. The start can be intimidating, and the obstacles along the way are sometimes challenging, but in time the process of gardening becomes an endless and beautiful experience. In this lovely book Mark Bolton explains his process in creating his ideal cottage garden and the rewards that have come to him. After observing and photographing gardens all over the world, he has developed a discerning eye and it is inspiring to see what he has created in his little patch in the Devon countryside.

The choice of a cottage garden was natural for Mark, around his nineteenth-century cottage, but this style of gardening is so versatile that it can work in almost any situation. Our plantings at Gravetye, in the garden of a grand old manor house, are often described as 'cottage garden style'. Here the free and naturalistic plantings contrast with formal architecture to create a magical landscape originally conceived by William Robinson over a hundred years ago. But while cottage gardens are usually associated with the countryside, it is in the urban environment that they are at their most valuable. Cottage garden plantings can create a haven of peace within bustling cities for people and wildlife alike.

The very phrase 'cottage garden' immediately conjures evocative images: the romance of Thomas Hardy's Wessex; informal gardens, full of flowers, humming with insects, organized yet charmingly chaotic. The style has many attributes, which have established its enduring popularity over the centuries. The aspect that I find most appealing is that a true cottage garden is a gardener's garden in its purest form, where the greatest quantity of favourite plants can be grown in the simplest way, and the gardener can play with careless care.

Tom Coward,
Gravetye, November 2023

Opposite Sea holly (*Eryngium planum*) grows well at Bowhay, and the birds and bees love it

Introduction

In 2021 we moved into a new – to us – house in deepest Devon. The oldest part is two hundred years old, the newest a mere hundred. It's in a small and (very) vibrant village in a farming area and there's nothing remotely grand or 'chocolate-box' about it. The interiors of the house lack ornament but, as with all cottages like this, it has beams and wonky walls, uneven floors and ridiculously low doorways – to which the frequent bumps on my head bear witness! There were the vestiges of a cottage garden at the back of the house, but most of it was just a rough lawn surrounded by a border containing overgrown shrubs, some rather moth-eaten roses and a handful of poorly-looking trees at the edges. There was, however, a rather ugly but useful potting shed that looked a bit like an Anderson shelter, and a gorgeous hawthorn that I could see immediately was very much home to a menagerie of sparrows, blue tits and starlings.

Despite the fact that the house itself needed masses of work, I felt that my first job was to overhaul the garden. The truth is that I itched to get out there and create my own little paradise.

I have been a garden photographer for more than twenty-five years, and the idea that the garden could become my outdoor studio was a temptation too strong to ignore. I have taken photographs of all sorts of gardens: big, small, modern, old-fashioned and everything in between; but there is no question, in my mind, that the most photogenic of all are the cottage gardens. Overflowing, billowing borders with eye-catching features in the background, borders filled with self-seeders that seem to pop up in just the right place (more about that later), and with a refreshing lack of respect for what colours do, or don't, clash. An idyllic and atmospheric little patch that I could shoot whenever I wanted and that would provide hours of interest. (And keep me fit, of course!)

I must emphasize however, that I never wanted to create a pastiche of a picture postcard garden; times have moved on, and many gardeners today are making cottage gardens with a modern twist, using, for example, grasses that fill the gaps in late summer, and even including areas of more formal design, such as a parterre. I want something too that still has interest in autumn and winter. It needs to be a garden with up-to-date planting, but with respect for the cottage garden's deep roots in history. These days most of us don't have a pig in the back garden, and many of us can afford to buy plants from the nearest garden centre; nevertheless, in these uncertain times, a return to the countryside, or even simply to 'the back garden', to till the earth, make our own food and just to potter is very alluring. The next chapter will deal with the history of the cottage garden, and how, over the centuries, what was traditionally seen as a rather dishevelled mixture of flowers, vegetables, compost heaps, chickens – and those pigs – became a 'style'.

As a photographer, I want my garden to be somewhere I can go to every day, in every season. I will try to show you how to plant in succession and how to plan ahead, so that we get spring tulips followed by roses in summer, autumn colour and texture, and then snowdrops in winter. I will try to give lots of advice about maintenance and seasonal jobs, tell you what is happening in my own garden as the year progresses, and show you some other gardens that are, to my eyes, inspiring. I must emphasize that I am not a professional gardener; I'm just a keen amateur, with no experience other than years of looking closely at plants and gardens for my work as a photographer, and years of making many mistakes, and some good choices, in my own gardens. I will also give some seasonal tips on what to photograph in your garden, and how to improve your skills. Most of all, I just hope you get inspiration from some of the great gardens I go to, and perhaps a tiny bit from my own efforts in Devon.

So, without further ado, let's take a look at what led up to what we now see as a 'traditional' garden style, and how we can make a garden of our own without too much outlay and just a bit of effort. Not to mention how we can make it a place that we want to be in, and – perhaps more importantly – that the birds and bees, and all the other wildlife, want to be in too.

A view from inside Beth Tarling's potting shed, looking at her wonderful cottage garden in summer

What is a cottage garden?

What actually is a cottage garden? Historically, it seems the term first appeared in literature in around the mid-eighteenth century, and after that, as the lot in life of the peasant worker changed and slowly got better, the idea of the romantic 'cottage garden' developed to become as much a 'style' as a fact. What had been a place where poor labourers grew their own food, their own medicines and their own decorative flowers became eventually a lifestyle choice. Essentially, though, the cottage garden was, and still is, 'a plot of one's own', filled with flowers and vegetables, useful and productive, a place to potter and a place to relax. It's usually a smallish plot characterized by a jumble of simple plants that fill the space in an undesigned way; there are no rules, there is no pomposity and anyone can do it. It's haphazard, homespun and humble. There will likely be recycled and reclaimed features, a mixture of simple flowers, some annual and some perennial, vegetables, herbs, climbers and wild flowers. It will probably have a romantic feel, some hidden corners, a higgledy-piggledy path, a pond and some rustic plant supports. The shed will be filled with saved seeds, old tools and a pile of terracotta pots. It's a haven for wildlife and it's a haven for the gardener, somewhere to escape the daily grind and get your hands dirty.

So then, let's look at the history of the cottage garden. In medieval times, the workers on large agricultural estates were housed in pretty much hovel-like cottages that had a tiny patch of land on which the 'peasants' would grow a selection of herbs and vegetables. The diet of these peasants was rudimentary, and meat, which was more than likely beyond their reach, was largely replaced by a narrow range of vegetables. During Elizabethan times, availability of vegetables increased and the cottager even started growing flowers, sometimes to mask the smells of daily life, but also for pleasure. Hollyhocks and sweet williams, for instance, became popular. As the eighteenth century approached, migrants,

largely from mainland Europe, brought in new types of plants, including different vegetables and a greater range of flowers. These migrants had hybridized plants to improve their form and performance, and as a result, particularly in the north of England, competitive showing of these saw the beginnings of the village flower and produce shows. 'Florists' societies' were common, with cottagers competing for best polyanthus, pink or pansy.

At the end of the eighteenth century, the 'rural idyll' began to gain traction with the Romantic poets and artists who moved away from increasingly dirty cities. Wordsworth and Coleridge, for instance, filled their cottage gardens with foxgloves and buttercups and began swapping seeds with their neighbours; we owe much of our 'cottage garden' tradition to these poets.

By the mid-nineteenth century, William Morris too had eschewed grimy industrial city life and set up home in the countryside. He was an environmentalist, a gardener, a designer, a poet – and a forerunner of the 'back to nature' movement. His first country garden at The Red House was a series of small garden rooms, filled with climbers and scented flowers. In other words, a set of connecting 'cottage gardens'.

Above, left Sweet williams (*Dianthus barbatus*)

Above, right Foxgloves (*Digitalis purpurea*)

Both at Bowhay House

Above Gravetye Manor gardens in September, its glorious tiled summerhouse surrounded by billowing borders

Then we come to William Robinson and Gertrude Jekyll, as formidable a pair of gardeners as you could imagine. These two did more than anyone to establish and modernize the idea of the cottage garden. In the early and mid-Victorian periods, the predominant style of gardening was formal, with bedding planted each year in rows of garish colour and uniform height. These large beds would perhaps be punctuated with 'focal points' of tender and exotic plants. The whole show needed lots of labour (planting out in rows, deadheading, then ripping it all out in autumn) and it needed greenhouses to bring on the bedding. William Robinson, in particular, hated this style of gardening and, along with Gertrude Jekyll, revitalized the idea of the 'cottage garden', the complete flipside of the bedding plant gardens. William had been trained in formal horticulture but had quickly rebelled, and his brilliantly practical and enthusiastic championing of the 'wild garden' through his books and magazine articles revolutionized gardening. He loved wild plants, bulbs, climbers and self-seeded annuals, and believed that gardens should be much more reflective of nature and the natural landscape. The garden he made at Gravetye Manor in Sussex became, and remains today, a mecca for cottage

Left The garden at Gravetye Manor today **(clockwise from top left)**: angelica stands sentinel among spring tulips; following in the footsteps of William Robinson, Tom Coward has taken on the role of Head Gardener; *Persicaria orientalis* hangs over *Dahlia* 'Magenta Star' in the late summer border; the walled garden, filled with vegetables, flowers and fruit

gardeners. He oversaw a return to the use of perennials to give structure and longevity to a border. Among these he allowed self-seeded annuals to appear. And he planted thousands of bulbs, including 100,000 daffodils alongside one of the lakes at Gravetye in 1897. His two most important books, *The Wild Garden* and *The English Flower Garden*, cemented his reputation.

He first met Gertrude Jekyll in 1875 and they had a close friendship and professional association for more than fifty years. He helped her with her garden at Munstead Wood in Surrey (well worth a visit); and she provided many of the plants for his garden at Gravetye Manor. Robinson's reputation cannot be overstated. His prolific (and vehement) writing and, above all, the garden that he built at Gravetye are testament to his standing as the father of the modern cottage garden. The garden is now watched over by the brilliant Tom Coward, who has taken over and modernized it, adding new planting and more modern varieties, such as tender salvias, persicaria, the sunflower *Helianthus* 'Lemon Queen', *Dahlia* 'Magenta Star' and *Kniphofia rooperi*. He has also given the kitchen garden a makeover (much of its produce is used in the restaurant of the Gravetye Manor Hotel).

Gertrude Jekyll became one of the most famous and lauded of all garden designers, and alongside the hundreds of gardens she made, she wrote several books and a thousand or so articles for eminent magazines. She was particularly known for the colours she wove into her borders, the hard landscaping she used to show off the plants, and the craftsmanship on which she placed enormous emphasis. She designed gardens for the new wealthy middle classes based on what she had seen as she grew up: small thatched cottages with climbers around the door, and borders stuffed with flowering plants, including annuals, biennials, bulbs and, of course, roses. She organized the colours, though, and, importantly, she mixed plants with different flowering periods to ensure non-stop bloom from spring till autumn.

As we enter the twentieth century, the story of the cottage garden continues at East Lambrook Manor, with its owner, another formidable plantswoman, Margery Fish. During the late 1930s, Margery and her husband arrived in a small village in Somerset from London, and they set about making a new garden around the old manor house. A novice gardener at the time, Margery went on to become one of the great plantswomen of the twentieth century, using her plot to save many traditional cottage garden plants,

and breeding many new ones as well. There are numerous plants that bear her name or that of her home (among them *Penstemon* 'Margery Fish' and *Euphorbia* 'Lambrook Gold') and the nursery at East Lambrook is well known for its variety of cottage garden favourites. The garden is again a collection of small 'rooms', all held together with a tapestry of densely planted herbaceous perennials, ground cover and self-seeding annuals. The borders are underplanted with bulbs, and there is a particularly impressive show of snowdrops in late winter and early spring.

During and after the Second World War, as a new austerity set in in Britain, Margery realized that gardening on a domestic scale needed to be more low maintenance; and she had already found that a good hardy perennial almost looked after itself. Under her influence, an informal cottage garden, mixing the old classics with some new modern plants, was born. Gardens such as Hidcote and Sissinghurst were already using the cottage garden style, but Margery's development was different because of its domestic scale. Visitors easily understood how it could relate to their own gardens. A visit to her garden, which has been developed further by the current owner, Mike Werkmeister, is a joy, particularly in

Above, left A fine show of snowdrops at East Lambrook Manor, one of the great twentieth–century cottage gardens

Above, middle images East Lambrook Manor during early summer: blurred edges, soft planting and the warmth of old stone

Above, right Bowhay House:
a work in progress

early summer, when geraniums, penstemons, salvias and nepeta
spill over and colonize the crooked paths that wind through the
borders. The air is full of the scent of flowers and the sound of
bees. Though Margery's garden has an old-fashioned air to it, with
the Hamstone sixteenth-century manor house catching the sun
and billowing planting softening the clipped yews, it is also a truly
modern garden. The plant nursery is bustling, and the tea house is
filled with contented tea-drinkers.

As we come into modern times, the cottage garden still thrives
and the uncertainty of the days we live in has given it new life.
The return to nature, the desire for a cosy home and a productive
garden, and the need to escape wall-to-wall social media and
rolling news have led to a resurgence in gardening; getting out into
the garden, feeling the soil between your hands and the sun on
your face, are greatly beneficial to us all, from the viewpoint of both
physical, and mental health. I can think of no better way to start
the day, or finish it for that matter, than planting seeds, weeding a
border or deadheading a rose. And whether you do that in a garden,
a tiny backyard, or even on a windowsill, hardly matters.

Try it.

A midsummer border
at Gravetye Manor, with
cottage-style planting
of aquilegias, lupins and
alliums that spill across
a paved path

Getting started

I have been photographing gardens for many years: chic town gardens, grand country house gardens with deep double borders, formal Italian gardens with statues round every corner, and somewhat eccentric gardens with gnome collections and follies built from reused wine bottles. However, what I really love to shoot, and what I will always make time for, is a cottage garden – billowing, colourful borders alive with bees and scent, dotted through with focal points: rose arches, fences, rustic hazel wigwams, old tin baths filled with summer colour and, of course, a productive vegetable patch next to an impossibly pretty potting shed.

When I recently moved to a nineteenth-century cottage in Devon, I finally had the opportunity to create my own version. So, in this book, I will show you how even an amateur gardener like me can make a decent stab at a new cottage garden, worthy of spending lots of time in, and perhaps, slightly selfishly in my case, worthy of taking pictures in – my job but also my passion!

So, let's get started. First things first, we need to look at the basic framework of the garden we already have and make some plans.

Assess the garden

The first rule of any new garden project is to sit back, wait and watch to find out what you've inherited. It's a mistake to pile in, all guns blazing, only to find you've planted a new hydrangea on top of the dormant remains of a group of glorious hollyhocks. So, if your plot is new to you, wait a year, and see where any bulbs might emerge in spring and what perennials or self-seeded annuals bloom in the summer. Although you will be keen to get on, having patience will give you a better picture of the space and allow for keeping any plants that work well – plants aren't particularly cheap, and the thrifty cottage gardener reuses and recycles.

Spend time in your patch. Check where the sun rises and sets and look for those spots where the sun hits just in time

for morning coffee or an evening drink. Find the shady areas
and look at where the shadows fall. Some plants prefer full sun,
others shady cool. Take a look at the boundaries too: stone walls
and rustic fences are typical cottage garden features and make
perfect supports for climbers and ramblers – very little looks as
pleasing as a honeysuckle in full bloom clinging to an old stone
wall. Notice any shrubs or perennials that you want to keep and
where the bulbs appear in spring and be sure to label them, as –
and I speak from experience – you will never remember them all. A
gardener's notebook can be useful to keep track of your plot, as can
photographs – you can even use your phone's camera to document
the space.

Remember that a shrub or perennial that has outgrown its space
may still shine elsewhere – or you could simply try to prune or
shape it rather than remove it.

Get to know your soil: you can buy soil-testing kits for a song
and they're invaluable in establishing whether you have an acidic
or alkaline soil. Also, get down on your hands and knees and grab
a handful of the good stuff – how does it feel? Sandy? Heavy with
clay? Ideally everything would be neutral but, if not, there are

Above, left and middle Two views of the garden on the day we moved in

Above, right Mark using a hosepipe to lay out the shape of a new border

plants which thrive in acidic or alkaline soils – it's just a question of working out which ones are right for yours.

Design the garden

Of course, the original cottage garden wasn't really 'designed' in the conventional sense; as it evolved from the need for a productive garden, plants were pretty much popped in wherever there was a space. In the nineteenth century, though, two great gardeners, William Robinson and Gertrude Jekyll, took the idea of the cottage garden and developed it to become a particular and recognizable style with its own set of requirements (although these are not rigid). To achieve the look in your own garden, some degree of design work is therefore a very good idea.

Once you have patiently waited to see how your space works and what is already there, it's time to think about how you'd like to change it to make it your own. Gather ideas together and make some rough plans. Study books and magazines, scour Pinterest and Instagram, watch TV programmes (yes, even those afternoon half-hour jobs where they say they can change a garden completely in two days!) and ideally visit some open gardens for inspiration.

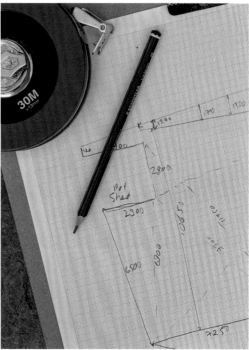

Map your space: try to transpose what is already there on to some paper, leaving in anything you're keeping – such as shed, patio, significant trees and shrubs, fences, gates and paths; and then add in any new things you'd like to incorporate. It's easy for me to say nonchalantly 'map your space', but I actually found this part incredibly difficult. You may have an idea of the shape of the garden in your head – square, for example, or long and narrow – but this can be surprisingly misleading. Having laboured away over a piece of graph paper for a couple of days, I eventually resorted to Google Maps and discovered that what I thought was a square garden was actually an oblong!

After measuring (using lengths of string and bamboo canes stuck in the ground at significant spots), I finally drew a scale map of the garden on a sheet of A3 paper; I found that working with a pad of tracing paper meant that I could revise and redraw the space many times. Once you have a design, keep looking at it, revising as necessary, but sticking to the general idea that you have laid out on paper.

Above A new cottage garden needs some design. Forethought and planning will save time and mean fewer mistakes in the long run

Build the garden

When it comes to putting your carefully drawn plan into action, the first step is the hard landscaping – any paths you want to add, new

Below Carefully positioning
some plants that will help form
the structure of the new bed

boundaries, patios or, that most useful of additions, the garden shed. Be sure to factor in any areas you will need for compost bins, tool stores and so on.

My garden has a simple design consisting of an X-shaped set of paths with new beds created within the triangles. The original borders, which I have kept, are around three sides of a central lawn that I carved up to give me more space for growing. Paths have a purpose, getting you from one part of the garden to another – in my case, diagonally from potting shed to compost heap and, on the other axis, from the back door to a sunny corner which always captures the last of the day's rays. The new central beds were edged with treated timber and on one side with a woven willow hurdle. A useful path will be a wheelbarrow's width, but a more carefree and indeterminate path could be just a linking series of stepping stones. The important considerations are where it's leading and how heavily it will be used. I settled for grass paths, and while they can wear quickly in wet weather, it's quite a traditional cottage look with its flourishing daisies and clover, both of which are adored by me and the bees. I have an extra grass path next to the back of the house

which is much used, so I have reused some old slate paving stones as stepping stones to protect the turf.

A path is also an opportunity to lead the eye, so I encouraged this with two metal arches planted with roses. A classic look – and there's very little more photogenic than a rose-covered arch in a cottage garden. Other focal points to consider carefully are containers, bird baths, water features or garden furniture. A cottage gardener would traditionally have made do and mended, so you will find a lot of holey watering cans and old tin baths used as plant containers.

I built a patio area using recycled bricks rescued from a friend's dismantled chimney, and this spot is perfect at the end of a summer evening, sharing drinks with friends and neighbours; it is now also home to a young wisteria which I hope will enjoy the sunny position.

In terms of tools required, I believe that a good set of hand tools is really all you need. Even though I have an electric hedge trimmer, I find that I will reach for my hand shears even more readily. I bought a stainless steel spade in good condition from my local council tip for just £5, but a set of well-made hand tools (buy the best you can) will last a long time. My red-handled secateurs are perfect and I have learned to sharpen them, thanks to YouTube. Boring as it may sound, time spent cleaning tools, sharpening and oiling them is well spent.

Plant the garden

Now, for the best bit – the plants. You have read, thought, dreamed and planned, you have built the paths and borders, and found space for the perfectly sited garden bench. Now it's time to populate the garden with the stars of the show. A good cottage garden probably peaks in midsummer, but, as you will see if you ever visit any of the great examples, such as Gravetye Manor in Sussex or East Lambrook in Somerset, the show can go on all year round.

To achieve a garden that looks good through the seasons, you need to think in terms of successional planting, so that as one plant fades, another is coming to take its place. The tulips, for example, are followed by the acid-green lady's mantle, towered over by stately alliums. The change of seasons, from late summer to early autumn, will then see the star-like blooms of asters, heleniums and dahlias bringing in some welcome colour and form.

As the original cottage gardens weren't much planned out, the planting can occasionally seem random, but all gardeners know that self-seeded plants need 'editing', and a structure of some sort needs to be in place before allowing the plants to do their thing.

Right Even in the first year, you can achieve some fabulous colour with plants you have grown yourself. In the garden at Bowhay we have already enjoyed many plants, including (*clockwise from top left*): `Pheasant's Eye' daffodil; Welsh poppy; *Dahlia* 'Park Record'; opium poppy

There are no hard edges here. The abundant planting – of varying heights – in this cottage garden really invites you in

A framework of shrubs and permanent perennials provides that structure, while the annuals and self-seeders can 'fill in the gaps'. My own garden is small, but there's room for a few roses, hydrangeas – and as I write this I am looking out on a little crab-apple tree, which will eventually give height. Then, perennials such as phlox, sedum, geraniums and astrantias will bulk up over the years to add the next layer. These can usually be divided every few years to provide more plants or replace those that have lost their lustre. Gap-filling annuals and biennials can change every year and are easily grown from seed sown in spring. I'm lucky to have a small potting shed with plenty of light, so I fill up dozens of seed trays.and other containers.

Beneath this layer are the bulbs that push their way up in spring, signalling an end to winter, while summer- or autumn-flowering bulbs that sit in the ground surprise even the most observant gardener by suddenly appearing as if out of nowhere – alliums, lilies, nerines and camassias will provide explosions of colour that can also smell heavenly. These bulbs really need to be planted while you're in the early stages of the garden build, so that 'drifts' of flowers will swirl around perennials, or nudge through annuals.

The original cottage gardeners were a generous bunch and plants were swapped and given freely, or grown from salvaged seed. Later in this book, I will show you how to save seeds and plant them up. Thrifty cottage gardening can be fun, and there is nothing quite like the feeling of planting out a group of annuals or perennials that you have grown from seed, especially if the seeds were a gift from a gardening friend. In the old days, most gardens were filled with standard 'common or garden' plants, rather than the fancy varieties that we can buy today from our local garden centres.

The lesson here is that there needs to be some planning if you want your garden to work through the seasons, so that there is always something to look at, delight in, and perhaps photograph. As I built my own garden, I was cutting out the new borders during autumn, mulching roses and also buying bulbs for the following spring (by the way, you can never order too many bulbs so, if in doubt and funds allow, double the quantity).

I kept the original borders of my garden which contained some old perennials: roses, phlox, salvias and euphorbias, so I was dividing and propagating these at the same time as popping in the perennials that I brought from my previous (seaside) garden. There was a cutting from a honey spurge that I had nurtured from a tiny plant, and alongside this, I built willow hurdles for one of my new borders.

As winter progressed, I was thinking longingly about summer – planting bulbs and erecting arches, cutting hazel branches for a plant support to be built in the spring – always planning ahead and enjoying the promise of what was to come.

We will talk a lot more about building the border and achieving a cottage garden style, but one last thought about plants. Plants respond to their environment and will not thrive unless they have the right amount of light and nutrients and are happy in their position. Beth Chatto, one of the great gardeners, always said that you need the 'right plant in the right place'. You can't grow a sun-loving lavender in a shady bog garden. So, read up about the plants you want to grow and the ones that you are given. Will they enjoy the conditions you can provide? A happily self-seeded plant is a prime example of 'right plant, right place', growing there because the place suits it. I will try and help you distinguish between different seedlings: which ones to keep – perhaps moving to somewhere else in the border – and those you may want to get rid of – I'm thinking bindweed, for example. Self-seeding is a joy, giving you new plants for nothing. However, we do need to 'edit', as they can take over. I have more *Verbena bonariensis* than I know what to do with.

Above A self-seeded angelica that has been allowed to stay among the lupins brings real drama to this border

Right This small cottage garden in London shows what you can do with an urban patch

Although it's a fabulous late summer filler, I am rigorous about pulling out any that are in the wrong place. These can be re-sited, or just composted (another important subject that I will discuss later).

Grow the garden

So, we have planted our garden and now we can relax and sit back and watch it do its thing – right? Not in the least: we have only just begun. If you're like me, you will probably have made more than your fair share of mistakes, and the next year or two will reveal them – maybe you have changed your mind on the colour of something, or realized that a plant has grown much taller than you thought. So, take a long hard look as each season progresses and make a list of what's needed. Having made a few purchases in year one, I decided to try to either propagate or swap as much as I could for year two. I bought an excellent book on propagation, took cuttings galore, divided perennials and collected as much seed as I possibly could. I have bulked up my stock of plants and, having carefully noted the look of different seedlings as they emerge in the garden, I have learned to leave certain plants that have now become a healthy population of foxgloves, verbascums and poppies.

In my day job I get to visit a lot of beautiful gardens, and I have made it a mission to ask as many questions and learn as much as I can from the experts. Visit gardens. The gardeners that you will meet are a lovely bunch, and keen to impart helpful advice for nothing.

So, let's don our wellies, grab the secateurs and weeding bucket, and get gardening! In this book, I hope to enthuse you and show you how to get started and learn the basics; I'll show you some inspiring cottage gardens and we'll discuss why they work, how they work and, most importantly, how you can easily and fairly quickly create your own garden paradise, no matter how big or small your plot. And, as a professional garden photographer, I'll give you some tips on how to photograph the results of your labour.

Right An aerial view of my garden in the first summer, showing the shape of the newly cut central beds

Through the seasons

SPRING IN THE COTTAGE GARDEN

Spring in full bloom
at Bowhay House,
with calendulas,
tulips and forget-
me-nots taking
centre stage

A snapshot of spring at Bowhay House

It's starting to feel like spring at last, as I sit here in the cottage to begin writing this. The acid-green alexanders (*Smyrnium olusatrum*) are just appearing in the lane outside the house, a bit later than usual this year, I think, perhaps because of the cold and rather damp start to the year. And at the top of the retaining wall that keeps the sheep in the field above from falling into the lane, the green shoots of valerian (*Centranthus ruber*) are sprouting beneath the brown crown of last year's stems. I wonder how many years this wall has looked the same; pennywort's umbilical leaves fill the gaps between the stones, just as they always have, and alexanders line the bottom, replaced by another umbellifer, hogweed (*Heraclium sphondylium*), later in the year. The road would once have been a rough farm track used by horses and carts – there's an old black and white print in the local pub of 'The First Car in the Village'! Nowadays cars park around the village green and the field is filled with campers during summer.

In the garden at the back of the house there is also new green growth, and drifts of daffodils and emerging tulips have forced their way through cold ground. I can hear skylarks too, whirring away in the sky above the fields, and I am, as ever, anxiously awaiting the arrival of swallows and 'our' house martins. They are usually here by the first week of April.

The two angelica plants (*Angelica archangelica*) that I planted last year have erupted this spring; they are biennial and put on a flowering spike in their second year, and I worry that they may actually grow to be too big. Like a pair of cuckoos, they appear rather ungainly. They will come into their own, though, during summer, when the large flower heads emerge, attracting insects. The old cottage gardeners would swear by angelica's medicinal value in treating all manner of ailments, from rheumatism to epilepsy. It also had uses in the kitchen, mostly as a sweet

substitute for rhubarb, or candied for cake decoration. (And young children would use its hollow stems as pea-shooters!)

All the roses have a healthy-looking burst of new foliage, and the 'chop' that I gave them during late autumn seems to have reinvigorated them. I am hoping that the climbing roses I planted on my new metal arches last year will actually climb a bit this year. I only planted them last spring, as bare-root roses, so they have not been hard-pruned, and all I have really done is tie-in any of the long stems so that there is some form of structure. It would be nice to see some real growth this year; last year I had to plant sweet peas to cover the arch a little. At the base of the roses, and in fact spread throughout my garden, are forget-me-nots (*Myosotis sylvatica*). Frothy sapphire-flowered clumps appear everywhere; and like many a good cottage garden flower, forget-me-not is a prodigious self-seeder that is easy to propagate. Simply dig up new seedlings and replant somewhere else; they are virtually impossible to kill, and during early spring you will be glad to have them. They mix well with tulips and other bulbs, and seem to bind a border together. And, while on the subject of self-seeders, I have discovered another plant that comes up here, there and everywhere. Hairy

Above, left Sheep in the field over the lane

Above, right Red valerian growing in the stone wall opposite our house

Above, left Angelica reaching skywards

Above, right Borage plants hidden among the forget-me-nots

bittercress (*Cardamine hirsuta*) is a wild plant in the same family as mustard. I rather like the look of it, and there are a few groupings near the shed, but it can, unfortunately, be a bit of a nuisance. The plants have an explosive seed dispersal mechanism which ensures that they get everywhere. The best way to deal with superfluous seedlings is by pulling them up or hoeing them. (No chemicals are used here, and we deal with 'weeds' by hand.) Hairy bittercress is in fact the food plant for a number of hoverflies and butterflies, so if you can leave a few in the ground, then you're doing nature a favour. Mine look rather lovely between the paving stones, but I'm keeping a keen eye on them. Lady's mantle (*Alchemilla mollis*), another classic cottage garden plant, is also peeping up from between paving stones, and the foliage, which is slightly cup-shaped when young, holds raindrops or the early morning dew.

The sun, which manages to come out from behind the clouds occasionally, is now beginning to feel a bit warmer, and is bringing on all the seedlings in the garden, and in the shed, which are heaving with trays full of promise. It's like a parking lot in the conservatory ('conservatory' is rather a misleading expression, it's actually a plastic lean-to at the moment), and there is a lot of

shunting around as I try to make room for new trays of cosmos, sunflowers, tithonia and tomatoes. I have fifteen 'Tigerella' tomatoes on the go and they are now 7.5 cm/3 inches tall; they sit alongside a small grouping of chrysanthemum cuttings that I took from a fabulous plant that my friend Beth Tarling gave me. I have a group of ipomoea seedlings that are doing reasonably well, but I have noticed that they seem to wither every time the back door opens. They are, I have discovered, rather susceptible to draughts (of which there are many in the plastic lean-to). And, at the moment, I have trays of *Tagetes* 'Cinnabar', with its second set of leaves a fine filigree of promise. The burnt umber of the flowers in midsummer is among my favourite colours in the cottage garden.

I'm in the garden very early this morning and it's Good Friday, which falls early this year. The recent mow (first of the year) has given the grass paths a sharp edge which accentuates the lush greenness of the borders. I don't have much in the way of lawn here, but the paths are grass and I have decided to restrict my mowing this year, to encourage the wild flowers and the insects that benefit from them. So I will leave some edges unmown.

I have just spotted the first of the buds of the Welsh poppy (*Papaver cambricum*), hanging beneath the foliage, covered in fine hair. The borage (*Borago officinalis*) is also in bud, its clustered blue flowers ready to shoot up and attract the bees. It has unusual flowers of the most intense blue, which are used in salads and in drinks, as they have a delicate cucumber scent. At the moment, the sheer diversity of foliage in the borders is a joy. A single high-rise stem of columbine (*Aquilegia vulgaris*) is reaching for the sky, and beneath it is a mat of leaves that has a curious resemblance to the club in a pack of cards. I was worried about an apparent lack of this plant a month ago, but they seem to have all arrived at once; it's funny how a change in the warmth of the air, or perhaps a drop of extra rain, can bring on a plant.

The hollyhocks (*Alcea rosea*) that I planted last year are sending up new leaves, at the moment unaffected by the hollyhock rust that is in the garden. There is little you can do about this fungal disease, except to strip off the affected leaves and give the plants plenty of air. Get rid of any debris around the base of the plant and perhaps add a layer of mulch early in the season to try to keep the fungus at bay. It's worth making an effort with these majestic plants. If you can grow them successfully, there is little more exciting than the sight of a 3-metre/10-foot hollyhock plant in full bloom.

Left, clockwise from top left
Borage; Welsh poppy buds;
columbine flowers in full
bloom in late spring; hollyhock
seedlings being planted out

Above, left Grape hyacinths at
the base of a cottage garden
wall

Above, right Dog's-tooth violet
(*Erythronium* 'Susannah')

Beneath the cherry tree, hundreds of seedlings are appearing, the progeny of the intriguing 'Jack by the Hedge' (*Alliaria petiolata*). This plant is quite tall, with a simple white flower and the distinct smell of garlic (it's otherwise known as garlic mustard), and apparently fresh leaves make a good addition to sauces and salads. However, it is rather rampant. I like it growing at the back of the shady border, at the base of the stone wall, but I don't want it everywhere. So perhaps, this sunny Easter weekend, my number one job will be to get down on my hands and knees and pull some of them out. They develop quite deep tap roots, so get them early, before they really settle in.

The stars of the cottage garden in spring

Let's start with the bulbs. A cottage garden in spring (in all seasons, in fact, but especially spring) isn't much of a garden without bulbs. Daffodils and tulips, hyacinths and fritillaries, there is such a range of plants that it's difficult to know where to start . . . Bulbs can be relied on to produce a burst of colour just when we need it most: after a long, dark and (certainly where I live) wet winter.

Little & large

My neighbour's house has an old stone wall with a fringe of grape hyacinths (*Muscari armeniacum*) that is invariably buzzing with early bees. They love it. These bulbs look wonderful en masse and they do spread quite quickly, so keep an eye on them. I have seen them at Keukenhof in The Netherlands planted in huge drifts, flowing like a river, and edged with tulips. Another classic cottage garden bulb is lily of the valley (*Convallaria majalis*). It is again a mall plant that spreads around, and it has the most wonderful fragrance and bell-shaped white flowers. It loves a shady spot and moist soil, so it will work well in my side border. Another possibility for the spring garden is the dog's-tooth violet (*Erythronium dens-canis*), a shade-loving bulb that likes to stay undisturbed and build up into large clumps. The species has a purple flower, but there are many varieties varying in shade from white to yellow and through to different pinks and purples.

At the other end of the scale, size-wise, are the crown imperial fritillaries (*Fritillaria imperialis*). Exotic, statuesque and a touch flamboyant, these bulbs, as big as your fist, erupt out of the early spring border in late March. They quickly head skywards and produce a rather crazy-looking crown of tubular flowers, which may be orange, red or yellow. They are an early introduction from Turkey, and quickly became a favourite in the cottage garden. They don't smell very nice, but their stateliness is welcome in the early border.

Daffodils

We shouldn't ignore the daffodil, of course, a host of which impressed William Wordsworth, one of the pioneer cottage gardeners. There are thousands of varieties of this bulb, in many forms and sizes, but all are yellow or white (except for the few which are orange!). The original cottage gardeners would probably have grown the native British 'Lent Lily' daffodil (*Narcissus pseudonarcissus*), but the choice nowadays is larger. I am fond of the classic small 'Tête-à-tête', which looks so good in containers or in drifts through a border, but I'm less keen on the garish yellow trumpets that seem to end up in petrol stations. After the plant has flowered, the foliage on these large modern daffodils is tricky to deal with and looks rather messy in the border for weeks. On the other hand, the late-flowering 'Pheasant's Eye' (*Narcissus poeticus*) is very attractive, with white petals and an orange centre, and looks perfect beneath trees.

Above, top Wild daffodil

Above, bottom Crown imperial

Right, clockwise from top left Tulip 'Spring Green' with tulip 'Slawa'; daffodil 'Martinette'; tulip 'Ballerina'; daffodil 'Pheasant's Eye'

On the whole, daffodils are fairly easy bulbs to grow, and can be left to their own devices once they are planted.

Tulips

Now, what about tulips? Leading us from spring into early summer, this huge group of plants comes in every form and nearly every colour. Elegant, perfect for the vase indoors and bringing a refined vertical accent to the border, they are eminently photogenic. It would be a poor excuse of a cottage garden that didn't include some tulips. They work brilliantly in pots, and can be excellent 'gap-fillers': for example, a pot of tulips popped into a space can suddenly 'lift' a section of border. I mix them with foliage (ferns, especially, look great with tulips) and build up spring displays. There are many varieties: if you choose carefully, you can keep the show going for weeks, and it's great fun choosing colour combinations: the classic 'Queen of the NIght', which is so dark it's nearly black, mixed with 'Purissima', an elegant white, is, for good reason, a famous combination. Many gardeners buy new tulip bulbs every year, as they tend to be less reliable after a year. I reuse the bulbs from my pots by just planting them around the garden. The resultant blooms are a bit hit and miss, but that's half the fun of a cottage garden: an accidental colour clash can sometimes work well, but if it doesn't, just pull them out and replant elsewhere.

Tulips get on famously with another cottage garden favourite, the wallflower.

Wallflowers

Wallflowers (*Erysimum*) can be biennial or perennial, the former being seeded in spring one year and then flowering the next, the latter best propagated by cuttings. They are all easy to grow, and there are many varieties and colours. I am particularly fond of one of the perennial varieties, called 'Bowles's Mauve'. It's easy to take cuttings from, and flowers pretty much non-stop. I even spotted some flowers at Christmas this year! The colour, a rich but subdued purple-mauve, makes it ideal as a backdrop to more showy plants, but the plant's shape makes it a focal point in its own right, perhaps at the end of a border.

Pulmonaria

Pulmonaria, commonly known as 'lungwort', is an interesting little groundcover plant often with speckled leaves (which probably

Left, clockwise from top left
Erysimum 'Bowles's Mauve';
Lamprocapnos spectabilis;
Kerria japonica; *Daphne bholua*
Jacqueline Postill'

Above, top The blossom of
apple 'Egremont Russet'

Above, bottom Buddleia
flowers

led to the belief that it could treat lung complaints, and hence its common name). It has nodding red, blue or white flowers that work well beneath many taller plants, and their early flowering makes them a welcome sight at the beginning of spring. Mix them with the common primrose (*Primula vulgaris*) for a heart-lifting spring sight.

Aquilegia

Columbine (*Aquilegia vulgaris*) is a traditional cottage plant that loves any old soil and thrives in a bit of sun. It's a rampant self-seeder, which means that once you have it, it will never leave you. The variations of colour are almost infinite; they cross-pollinate endlessly, and it's fun to guess what shade will come up next. They can be used as 'threads' that bind a border together. Where you want them, let them stay, running through, around, beneath and behind other plants; or pull them out and replant somewhere else.

Plants for shade

For the more shady areas of the garden, 'bleeding heart' (*Lamprocapnos spectabilis*) is a rather unusual-looking perennial with delicate foliage and long, arching stems tipped with heart-shaped flowers. There are pink and white varieties, and the old cottagers would call them 'Lady in a Bath', which is what you are supposedly able to see if you carefully pull back the petals and look closely. (I had a go and couldn't see the bathing lady at all!) They work very well with hellebore seed heads (hellebores are likely to be seed heads by the time *Lamprocapnos* flower), and the long stems die back in summer, leaving room for other plants.

Shrubs and trees

Shrubs and small trees are a mainstay in the cottage garden, giving structure and height to the border. As cottage gardens tended to be quite small, the cottager would never plant too many trees, and those that were planted had to earn their keep. Fruit trees obviously qualified, and in spring one of the most beautiful sights is fresh apple blossom. Be careful planting fruit trees though: they will be there a long time, and although dappled shade is welcome during summer, too much shade can be problematic. Choose carefully: trees that are on smaller rootstocks might be better, depending on how much space there is. It's best to buy from a reputable nursery that can tell you which variety, and which rootstock, will serve you best in your garden. My crab-apple is a variety called 'John Downie'.

Flowering shrubs can add early scent and colour: lilac, ornamental quince, forsythia, kerria and viburnum are all reliable and easy shrubs that flower in spring. *Daphne* 'Jacqueline Postill' has a phenomenal scent and is worth growing despite being a little 'particular'. It resents being moved and doesn't like frost, but it's worth the anxiety just for the smell on an early spring day. I have a shrub known as mountain pepper (*Tasmannia lanceolate*), which was here when we moved in, and as a backdrop to other plants in the border, it's perfect. It is evergreen, requires very little maintenance and in early spring it's covered in small creamy-white flowers. It sits at the back of the side border (one of the few areas which we have not changed), and is an unobtrusive but vital part of the structure. Shrubs like this really are worth their place: the backbone of the garden.

What to do in the spring garden

Spring, traditionally, was the time to start mowing the lawn. A seemingly endless task – it only takes a day or two after mowing for the grass to be clutching at your ankles again! Like many people nowadays, I try to leave some of it completely and let the grass and wild flowers that are hidden within grow for the summer. Over the last fifty or so years, we in Britain have lost about 97 per cent of our wildflower meadows – and, as a result, many of the insects and mammals that relied on them. However, the gardens of this country make up a significant area of land, and if we all encouraged the grass to grow and the wild flowers to bloom, we would do a lot of good for our biodiversity. The paths in my cottage garden are grass, and I have decided to just mow a line down the middle, leaving the grass at the sides to grow. We will see how it looks in late summer!

Tidying the garden

Tidying the garden moves up a gear at this time of year, and apart from the obvious weeding and mowing duties, do make sure that you cut off the spent flowers of daffodils, tulips and other early spring bulbs. This ensures that the plant directs its growth and vigour back to the bulb rather than into seed production, and means that you should get better flowering next year. Check that any permanent plant supports are in good shape; I have just retied the bindings around my hazel wigwam, and my low willow hurdle was in need of some TLC. Check any cold frames for pests; I had a single snail which had managed to remain hidden in the cold frame, during which

Right The grass growing at the edge of the paths next to the borders is filled with daisies

time it decimated a complete tray of marigolds. In the vegetable patch, broad beans will be shooting up; pinch out the tips of the plants if they're covered in blackfly, or spray shoots with soap-based solution. And while on the subject of aphids, now is the time to try and stop any infestations on the new soft growth of roses and any other susceptible plants (aphids seem particularly to love aquilegias). Rather than using chemicals, try some watered-down soapy water and wipe it around the buds and young leaves with your fingers.

'Weeds'

As the spring rolls in, so do the weed seedlings. Now, there is much to recommend many so-called 'weeds', and definitions of what a weed actually is tend to be unhelpful. If a weed is just a plant that is in the 'wrong' place, that could actually be a seedling of a much-loved phlox or poppy, but situated in the 'wrong' part of the garden. The cottage garden is pretty much a jumble of plants, so the idea of a plant being in the wrong place is a bit meaningless, but it's all about editing out. The early cottage gardeners loved buttercups and would allow and even cosset them. Be careful which buttercups you encourage though. The creeping buttercup (*Ranunculus repens*) is an invasive plant that will take over quickly, and although it's highly beneficial for insects, you'll be better off in your borders with the meadow buttercup (*Ranunculus acris*), which is much easier to stop in its tracks. Alongside the buttercups in my border is red campion (*Silene dioica*), another wild plant that thrives here, weaving its way around the hellebores and camassias in the shady area. But at this time of year, as unwanted seedlings appear in number, it's best to keep on top of the job, and pull them out or use a hoe around the border. I love the look of dandelions (*Taraxacum officinale*), and they are a valuable food source for many early moths and insects, but I prefer them in the lawn rather than in the borders, so I will dig them out (and try to get out all the long tap root, as even the smallest bit left in the ground will regrow). Weeding is a satisfying job, and I love the contemplative side to it, but, as with everything, there is a balance to be kept. Let the garden grow and allow some space for accidentals. And the bees will be pleased to see the lovely sunny faces of dandelions in the grass in early spring.

Right, clockwise from top left
Spray newly formed rosebuds with soapy water to deter the aphids; deadhead tulips; red campion (*Silene dioica*); and dandelions

Planting out seedlings

Spring is the time to start planting out some of the seedlings that you have been nurturing on the windowsill, but it's a bit of a balancing act. A young plant may look healthy and strong sitting on your windowsill, but if you put it straight outside, the chances are that it will struggle. Carefully check these signs to make sure that the plants are ready for moving outdoors. If the plant is roughly twice the height of the pot it's in, and at least as wide, then it will probably have used the nutrients in the pot soil (there is usually, at most, about eight weeks' worth of nutrient in each pot) and it will likely be drying out quickly too. Check if the plant is 'pot-bound' by carefully removing the pot and checking the roots. If they are starting to grow around the root ball, it's a sign they need more room. And if the leaves are starting to yellow, it probably means the plant is lacking nutrients. If the answer to any of these checks is 'yes', then it is time to move the plant into the border or to repot. The move outdoors is not just a case of plonking them into the ground and hoping they will take off just like that. Plants need a week or two of 'hardening off' to get them acclimatized to the wind and weather. Use a cold frame or a cloche to protect the young plants and get them used to being outdoors. Then, on a dull but warmish day, plant them in the border, water them in well and keep a close eye on them. Check the weather forecast and try not to do this if bad weather is imminent, as small plants are very delicate and young leaves are likely to break off if you are not careful.

Above Placing young snapdragon seedlings in a homemade cold frame

Sowing seeds

Spring is the optimum time to really get your seed-sowing regime under way. As the days lengthen and become warmer, you can begin sowing hardy annuals and vegetables straight into the ground. You can also start sowing half-hardy annuals (cosmos, tithonia, even dahlias, for example) and tomatoes or chillies under glass. Different seeds require different methods of germination, so it's important to read the seed packet. As a general rule, tiny seeds (poppies and aquilegias, for example) may just be sown on the surface and covered with, at most, a very fine vermiculite or grit; water them in well, using a fine mist spray to ensure you don't wash them away. Larger seeds should be pushed in at a depth approximately three times the size of the seed. When sowing directly into the ground, make a fine tilth in the seeding area and mark out the ground so that you know not to plant something else there. You can use small sticks or even a line of sand to show where the seeds have been planted. Firm down the ground with a rake and water in well. (Birds like eating some small seedlings, so you may have to protect them with fine netting until they establish.)

Plant supports

As the spring progresses, plants will suddenly burst forth and there will be a lot of new growth, which may need support, as young growth in plants doesn't have the strength of more established growth. The support you put in place could be simple stakes that you tie stems to, or perhaps more substantial supports that will last for the whole season – or even longer. This is a cottage garden, so rustic plant supports are entirely acceptable, and the original cottagers would have used twigs and branches from around the garden or surrounding countryside to support their sweet peas and runner beans. I raided a local woodland for some hazel stems for my garden, and they have been in place for two years, supporting summer growth and providing structure which looks good even in the depths of winter. I tied them together with thinner, more supple willow stems from the local pond. I have also used some rusted metal supports for the perennial plants that start their growth early in spring. It's a good idea to have the supports in place well before the growth really gets going, so that the plants naturally grow around and through the supports.

Softwood (basal) cuttings

Spring is a good time to take softwood or basal cuttings of many plants. There is a huge satisfaction in increasing your plant stock by taking cuttings; it's free and it's pretty easy to do. Perennial plants such as penstemons, anthemis, petunias and verbenas, and also some shrubs – such as hydrangeas – can be propagated in this

way, and your stock of delphiniums, lupins, dahlias and other seed-producing plants can be increased by basal cuttings.

Use a very sharp knife to take basal cuttings from the edge of the new growth that develops from a crown. Remove lower leaves to reduce water loss from the cutting. Quickly dip the end of the cutting into rooting compound and place it in a pot of new cutting compost. Then either cover the pot with a plastic bag or place it in a propagator to keep in the moisture. Rooting should happen within a few weeks. Place the cuttings in good – but not direct – light and make sure that you harden off any plants before placing them outside.

Seedlings in the borders

And, while I'm on the subject of increasing your stock of plants for free, do keep an eye on the new seedlings that are springing up in the borders. You will find that around established plants such as lupins, larkspurs and hollyhocks, there are often seedlings that you can carefully dig up and either move to a new position or simply pop in a pot and keep for later. You may not have the room at the moment, but gaps will appear and these transplants are perfect little 'drop-in' fillers.

Above, left Staking a young peony

Above, right Sowing sweet pea seeds

Right A healthy patch of ground in the shady spring border, jam-packed with all sorts of seedlings – some of which may have been described as weeds!

Planting bulbs for summer

Now is a good time to plant some summer bulbs. Lilies for example can be planted directly in the borders or in pots, and as long as they are planted two to three times as deep as they are in size, they will give you many weeks of colour and impact. If planting in pots (a good idea, I think, as they are excellent gap-fillers later in the summer when some of the early colour has disappeared), add some grit; most bulbs enjoy really good drainage. If you can, plant in groups of at least three to five, separated by the required amount of space so that they have room to grow. The more the merrier! Drifts of bulbs shooting up in the border are a sight to behold.

Cottage containers in spring

The borders in spring can sometimes be hit or miss; using containers is one way of ensuring that you still have a wonderful display. Place your container either in a key position that catches the eye, or simply right outside the door where you can best appreciate it. It seems obvious, but spring containers are all about the bulbs for me, and I generally go for simplicity when it comes to spring pots.

Above, left Lupin and larkspur seedlings that have been 'edited' out of the border

Above, right Basal cuttings of dahlias

A ROUND-UP OF SPRING JOBS

1 Plant summer bulbs to give an impressive display later.

2 Take softwood or basal cuttings from many perennial plants and shrubs.

3 Support plants with bamboo stakes or metal ring supports. Plants with heavy flower heads on new growth, such as peonies, especially benefit.

4 Sow seeds of hardy and some half-hardy annuals and vegetable plants.

5 Weed the garden regularly so that weeds don't get a hold. (But maybe leave some weeds that are beneficial to wildlife.)

6 Paint, varnish and refresh your outdoor furniture – which will preferably be wooden. A rustic, well-worn look is more in keeping with the cottage garden tradition than brand-new plastic – but wooden furniture will look better and last longer if you keep it maintained.

7 Keep on top of aphids and slugs by regular patrols around the garden. Use slug beer traps or soapy water for aphids. Regular and often is the answer!

8 Early spring is a good time to prune roses. Using a clean and sharp pair of secateurs, make a sloping cut about 6mm/¼ inch above an outward-pointing bud.

9 Look after the birds in your garden and feed them regularly as they are nesting. The best foods are fatballs, seeds and nuts from a nut feeder (but never leave out whole peanuts as they are just the right size to choke fledglings).

10 Leave out meat-based foods for hedgehogs and cut small holes in your fences so they can move about, getting rid of slugs and snails. Hedgehogs are definitely the gardener's friend.

A PROJECT FOR A SPRING DAY

Taking basal (softwood) cuttings

(clockwise from top left)

Cutting a basal shoot from a dahlia

Stripping lower leaves

Placing the cutting in a propagator

The cutting, tipped with rooting powder, being inserted into compost

Left Tulips 'Ballerina', 'Rococo' and 'Princess Irene' in a mixture of containers at Bowhay House

Above, left Tulip 'Spring Green'

Above, right Daffodil 'Martinette' with polyanthus and grape hyacinths

A ravishing show of colour co-ordinated tulips really does take a bit of beating! However, try mixing in a few other plants to add subtlety to the knock-out hit that daffs and tulips give; soft evergreens or foliage plants work well as backdrops to the main event, and you could even drop in a feathery grass behind the bulbs. For example, *Stipa tenuissima* works well behind grape hyacinths (*Muscari armeniacum*).

Bedding plants such as polyanthus and daisies are plentiful at this time of year, and a pot filled with zingy colour backed by a feathery fern is hugely satisfying. It's easy to get carried away with trying to pack lots of plants into large containers, but the original cottage gardeners would have used whatever they had in their gardens and perhaps kept to a collection of smaller pots. This way it's easy to swap things around and make a display: you could try, for instance, a couple of small pots of three tulips alongside a pot with an aeonium, and a fern or foliage plant as a counterpoint. And use recycled bits and pieces. I found a lovely old metal birdbath which is small enough to move around and this works well with my pots. An old broken teapot, or even a cup and saucer, cleverly placed, can get involved in the action.

Many spring containers include bulbs, and it's worth remembering that these will need to be planted in the autumn before. (You can, of course, buy bulbs that are already in flower in garden centres or nurseries, but that's a much more expensive way of doing things.) Spring bulbs flower at different times, so when planning a container, you can plant for successional flowering, layering the bulbs in the 'lasagne' style, whereby bulbs are planted at different depths so that the flowers come over a period of time. Perhaps crocus might flower first, then tulips or daffodils, finishing off with a late-flowering daffodil like 'Pheasant's Eye' (*Narcissus poeticus*). The alternative is to go for one big blow-out with everything flowering at once.

If you plant in layers, the larger bulbs should be the deepest, the smallest at the top, and each layer of bulbs should be separated from the next by a layer of soil about 7.5 cm/3 inches deep. Make sure that the containers have really good drainage, as most bulbs hate being waterlogged, and spring can often be wet. Place crocks of old broken terracotta pots over the hole at the bottom of the pot, mix some grit into the compost (at approximately a three to one ratio of compost to grit), and place the pots in as sunny an area as possible. If you worry about squirrels stealing the bulbs, you can place a piece of chicken wire over the pots until shoots begin to appear, and this should protect them. As the plants flower over the spring months, make sure that you deadhead regularly. This encourages more flowering and keeps the pots looking at their best. And, after all the flowering is finished, it's worth leaving the foliage until it goes yellow and dies off. This helps the plant replenish energy in the bulb, and these can then be replanted either in new pots or in the border, in the following autumn.

Above Daffodils in a recycled wheelbarrow 'container'

Right Pots containing tulips 'White Parrot' and 'Spring Green' placed in front of 'Ice King' daffodils

Left Spring planting in raised
beds at Seaview Cottage,
Cornwall

Below The garden at Seaview
Cottage is filled with spring
colour and is a wonderful
example of what can be
achieved in a sustainable way

An inspiring spring garden
Seaview Cottage, Cornwall

This is the garden of a friend of mine, Beth Tarling, an inspired
amateur gardener who is fascinated by the history of gardening and
has a collection of books, pots, tools and implements that would
frankly put many a museum to shame. The garden is simply arranged
in raised beds with straight paths between, and surrounded by
potting sheds that her partner, Dan, has built. Much of what is there
(including full sets of terracotta pots in every size imaginable, pre-
war seed packets, postcards and adverts for village flower shows
of the 1950s) has been acquired at car boot sales or found on the
internet. The garden in spring is a colourful and carefully curated
collection of tulips and daffodils, with terracotta pots filling every
gap. The greenhouse is stuffed with seedlings, and the benches
heave with homemade compost. Beth is an organic gardener, and
the compost heaps are, unlike mine, properly arranged and carefully
looked after; nothing goes to waste – and there is not a hint of
plastic. The garden is in a beautiful location with views of the sea and
it is open for the National Gardens Scheme. Well worth a visit.

What and how to photograph in spring

Photography outdoors is all about the light, and great garden
photography means getting up very early or staying out late. The
low-angled sun at either end of the day is what you are after: the soft,
but direct, sunlight can backlight or softly illuminate the details of a
glorious flower, or pick out different areas within a border. Look at a
great painting and see how the artist is using the sun to highlight areas
of interest in a view. This is what, in some small way, you are trying to
achieve. During spring, this softness of light may begin and end in an
hour or so around the dawn (which, luckily, at this time of year is later
than at midsummer). You get a similar effect in the evening before
dusk, but in my opinion there is nothing like leaving the house in the
dark and arriving at the place you want to photograph as the sun is
rising; if you can do this in your own garden, then all the better – you
don't have to set the alarm for quite so early!

In the spring border, look out for emerging bulb flowers. I love
Allium siculum and its rather oddly shaped flower heads as they start
to form. These will become bell-shaped flowers that are creamy-
coloured and flushed with purple, and later in the summer those same
bells turn the other way up as they become seed heads. So, all in all,

Above, left Raised beds,
vintage cloches and terracotta
forcing pots form the spring
structure at Seaview Cottage

Above, right Laundry drying on
the line at Seaview Cottage

Above, left Sicilian honey garlic (*Allium siculum*) photographed with a macro lens and showing in the background the effect of circular highlights (known in photographer's parlance as 'bokeh')

Above, right Look out for dewdrops clinging to the soft petals of tulips in early spring

a very photogenic flower. Get in really close with a macro lens and if you use a wide aperture on your camera, you can separate the detail from the background. And if you have speckles of bright light behind, you may get what is called 'bokeh', when the light spots form beautiful circular highlights.

Pots of bulbs, if you can lift them, can be moved into different positions so that the colours of the bulbs contrast with or complement the background.

Look out, too, for the drops of dew that form in early morning. These can look very striking as, clinging to the soft petals of a tulip, they catch the light of early spring.

While bokeh can be charming, most of us would generally wish to avoid lens flare. As light coming obliquely at a camera hits the lens, some of it can bounce off, instead of going into the lens. This causes flare, which reduces contrast and can cause 'flare spots'. (Actually, there is a current trend for including flare spots in images, and these can give atmosphere to a picture.) Here, it's worth thinking about the benefits of a lens hood. These crucial bits of kit stop (or at least reduce) flare. Sometimes, though, the easiest thing to do is to use your hand, positioning it just out of view and blocking the sun out.

TOOLS

Gardening techniques and practices have changed very little really since the days of the early cottage gardeners. Most gardeners still use the same type of tools that were around hundreds of years ago (although these days, unfortunately, more plastics and aluminium are used in their making). A good spade and fork for digging and lifting, a hoe for weeding, a rake and a hand trowel and fork are the basics, and, along with a pair of secateurs and some shears, this should suffice for most work in the garden. There are a few extras that help: a watering can and a wheelbarrow, for instance. Try to buy a metal watering can if you can (so much nicer than a plastic one, especially when photographing your garden).

During the quieter months of autumn and winter, one of my favourite gardening jobs is maintaining and looking after the tools in my shed. I am happy spending time sharpening and oiling the tools, so a good sharpening stone and a can of oil are worthwhile additions to any tool-shed, and these can, of course, be bought at most hardware shops. I always advise spending a bit more on your tools if you can (although, to be honest, I have found a good part of my kit by visiting the local amenity tip where the council has a shop selling the useful bits and pieces that people have thrown away). I have lost count of the number of cheap secateurs that I have broken, before I spent a bit more on a good-quality pair that can be sharpened and repaired easily and certainly feels better in the hand than the cheap ones that just fall to bits.

Tools are very personal, and you get used to them, in the same way that a carpenter might get used to his or her own chisels or plane. I guess what I mean is they should be bought with care and attention, and with the intention that they should last a lifetime.

Opposite My rather motley collection of garden tools, many of which I am fond of, even if they are a bit down at heel

Above If you buy good-quality tools and are prepared to spend time maintaining them, they can last a long time

EARLY SUMMER IN THE COTTAGE GARDEN

Foxgloves (*Digitalis purpurea*), *Cirsium rivulare* 'Atropurpureum', sweet william (*Dianthus barbatus*) and cornflowers (*Centaurea cyanus*) mix informally in the borders at Bowhay House in early summer

A snapshot of early summer at Bowhay House

I have staked the stately angelica and placed protective plant
supports around the burgeoning lupins and sweet rocket. The
'green fuse' of plant power is everywhere to be seen in the borders,
so much so that all the new growth needs a bit of support. Most
vigorous of all is the grass in the paths that intersect the garden. I am
trying out 'no-mow' May, and have left about 30 cm/12 inches along
each side of the paths where I will allow the grass and flowers to
grow unfettered for a month or so. Already I have been bowled over
by that most simple of flowers, the common daisy. It's everywhere
in the grass, alongside clover and dandelions, its perfect little face
beaming up at me. No fussy leaves, just a rosette of greenery with
sturdy stalks that support a flower with white petals radiating from
a butter yellow centre. The bees love it (as they do dandelions and
clover), and it makes you think, why do the stripey lawn brigade
hate it so? We have lost 97 per cent of all our wildflower meadows
in the last fifty years, and gardens in the UK could, and do, help to
ameliorate the massive loss in ecological diversity. I'd rather see and
hear the insects and watch the so-called 'weeds' thrive than have a
perfect striped lawn.

Some of the tulips are still just about hanging on, and aside from
any odd colour combinations (a result of the random planting in the
borders of last year's potted bulbs), they bring a tall and welcome
burst of early summer colour above wafts of frothy forget-me-nots
(*Myosotis sylvatica*). The camassia (*Camassia leichtlinii*) beneath
the bird box (which has already hosted one set of new blue tits) is
just flowering, and I can see that the crab-apple tree I planted last
autumn is clothed in acid-green new foliage. Dotted around the
garden are gangs of Welsh poppies (*Papaver cambricum*), mixed
among alliums galore. In fact, many more alliums than I remember
planting! The Sicilian honey garlic (*Allium siculum*) is looking ready to
burst out, and if I had to choose just one plant to photograph at this

time of year, it could well be this one. It's a slightly mad-looking bulb with fabulous little bell-shaped flowers on top of an incongruously skinny stem. The colour is an unusual mix of a pale purple and green, and to add to the fun, the individual seed heads turn upside-down when they are ripe.

It's early summer and I can't think of anywhere I would rather be than here in the garden, among the plants, coaxing, staking, weeding and planting. Or standing and gazing in wonder at what has just turned up. Try as you might, a gardener is never truly in control, and one of the joys of gardening is accepting that and working with nature rather than trying to beat it into submission.

The editing process continues, and some spring plants are now past their best and must be evicted from their spots to make room for others that are outgrowing their pots in the so-called 'nursery area' I have made in the corner of the garden. I can now plant out some of the larkspur and lupin seedlings I have nurtured – and even some borage seedlings, which, though it's ridiculously promiscuous, I have taken to my heart. It's a gangly and rather unruly plant, but it really has the most fabulous sapphire-blue flowers and is so easy to grow. There are also sunflowers which could do with planting out,

Above, left Sicilian honey garlic or *Allium siculum* (syn. *Nectaroscordum siculum*) just about to burst into flower

Above, right *A. siculum* in bloom on a dewy morning

Above The perfect spot for a morning coffee

and dahlias too. The last frost used to be thought of as around the date of the Chelsea Flower Show at the end of May, but down here in sunny Devon we can reasonably expect winter to be done by mid-May, so I am happy to take a risk. In fact, I always keep a few back in the potting shed 'just in case'. I am also tidying up some of the early daffodils and have found room for some bishop's flower (*Ammi majus*) where there had been a patch of persistently flowering deep orange marigolds – appropriately named 'Neon' if I remember rightly!

The roses are looking fabulous at the moment, and I think the combination of a careful prune in early spring and a nice thick mulch of compost has paid dividends. The plants that I inherited were looking old and a bit ragged, but the transformation this year has been incredible. There are many more blooms than last year and the foliage looks much healthier. I also planted some David Austin roses, which now seem to have bedded in, and 'Claire Austin' (a climber) is actually sending up some nice long shoots which are aiming towards the top of their arch. Roses are, of course, a must-have in the cottage garden, and they really do form the focal point around which other, less obvious plants play second fiddle. Catmint (*Nepeta* 'Six Hills Giant' is a favourite) is one of those, and in combination with almost any rose is an integral part of the English summer garden. There is also an unnamed rose which was looking rather leggy last year, and the happy accident of some self-seeded sweet rocket (*Hesperis matronalis*) beneath it has covered some of the bare branches and stems and given the blooms a setting above a beautiful frothy base.

The alliums have faded and will be seed heads soon, but there's plenty to take their place; hollyhocks are forming buds and are seemingly shooting up behind my back, and poppies of all types are in full bloom. The opium poppies (*Papaver somniferum*) are already 1.5 m/5 ft tall and forming new buds alongside their photogenic seed heads every day. There are 'Danish Flag' poppies which have improbably fringed red and white petals, and there is a rather amazing bright pink pom-pom headed variety too. These plants do have their problems, though. I need to stake them as, even in this sheltered garden, they are prone to wind damage and have brittle stems that grow so fast they have very little strength. The lower leaves are also quick to go brown, so I spend a lot of time clearing the debris beneath them. But mixed among other plants they look remarkable – and the companion plants help to shield the rather messy foliage.

Below, left Marigold (*Calendula*) 'Neon'

Below, right Bishop's flower (*Ammi majus*)

Right *Allium* 'Purple Sensation' (now going over), sweet william, foxgloves, roses and poppies sit well together in this cottage garden border

There are foxgloves everywhere through the borders, their tall spires giving an almost musical rhythm to the planting, and there are many white flowers among the more common pink. The noise of bumblebees visiting them can be deafening in the early morning, and mixed with the chit-chat of house martins swirling above, it's an invigorating blast of nature that accompanies me as I wander through the garden.

The honeysuckle (*Lonicera periclymenum*) which I planted against the black-painted shed is doing well, and the scent is heady as I stand in the doorway of the shed looking out at the tomatoes planted beneath the hazel wigwam. I noticed that some of the honeysuckle leaves had gone brown earlier and was rather worried they had a disease of some sort, but once I had given them a watering, they seemed to pick up. I suspect that the soil at the base of the shed is quite thin and will need some improvement over the autumn.

Across all the borders are a few stands of cornflower (*Centaurea cyanus*) which have self-seeded from last year's plants, and I love their ephemeral and transparent form. Even though they are quite tall and often at the front of the border, they are a little bit like the vervain (*Verbena bonariensis*) that comes later in the season in that they do not obstruct the view; the almost impossible blue of the flowers seems to float in front of you. I only wish I had more of them. I shall make a note to encourage more seedlings next year.

My only peony (*Paeonia lactiflora* 'Felix Crousse') has, as peonies will, flowered for its all-too-brief moment of glory. It managed two flowers this year, and a handful of buds didn't develop. I have read up on this and assume that it's because the plant is still young (two summers old) and that we had a dry spring. Apparently, the root system needs to develop for up to five years to support flowering, and they are rather susceptible to too much shade, too much rain – or lack of rain! As with all gardens, some plants do well, other don't, and differing conditions each year mean that it's normal to have a mixed bag of success and failure.

Above Mauve opium poppy (*Papaver somniferum*)

Above Cornflowers **(left)** and foxgloves **(right)** are both bee magnets in the garden

In the vegetable patch, the tomatoes are now well bedded in and producing a few fruit trusses. These are 'Tigerella' tomatoes, which are a vine-type plant, so there are a few important things to remember about growing them. The side shoots should be removed (unless you have 'bush' type plants), and it's important this is done regularly. The side shoots come out between the main leaves and the main stem, and they need to be removed so the plant can channel its energy into producing fruit rather than foliage. Once it has produced four or five trusses of fruit, the plant can be 'stopped' by pinching out the growing tip. This ensures that the fruit will develop and mature properly. And tomatoes respond well to being fed; they are hungry plants. They need good compost to grow in and an added feed as the fruit forms. I use organic liquid feed and buy it off the shelf, but many people have their own closely guarded secret recipes for making up a liquid form of fertilizer.

Alongside the tomatoes are a few broad beans that are now laden with pods. These are my very favourite vegetables and easy to grow. The flowers are much loved by the bees, and some varieties even have red flowers as opposed to the more usual white. They are fairly trouble-free and as long as you give them a bit of support and

pinch out any tips when the blackfly arrives (and it will!), you can guarantee a supply of beans throughout early summer. The aphids love the fresh green and soft tips of the plant, and if these are taken out, they seem to lose interest.

The stars of the cottage garden in early summer

Fragrant dianthus

Sweet williams and cottage pinks belong to the dianthus family, and are classic cottage garden favourites. Here they have been flowering their socks off for weeks. If you really get down low and take a proper look (get out a macro lens and photograph them closely), the petals have finely detailed patterning. Sweet william (*Dianthus barbatus*) is biennial – a two-year life cycle where you sow the seed one year and it flowers the next year – and has a fringed ruff beneath a flattened head of early summer flowers. It is easy to grow and best planted in drifts at the edge of the border. Cottage pinks (so called because the serrated edges of the petals look a bit like they have been cut with pinking shears) have grey-green foliage and are perennials. They have an amazing ability to look fresh when cut, even after weeks in a vase.

Left The 'Tigerella' tomatoes are having a growth spurt in the vegetable patch, among the foxgloves, poppies and lavender

Above Now is the time to begin harvesting the broad beans, alongside cut flowers and handfuls of herbs

Foxgloves and roses

Foxgloves are among the cottage garden stalwarts and are, of course, a British native plant; their spiked flower heads rise above the borders and are beacons for bumblebees. The flowers are usually dark pink with a spotted throat, but the white version is fabulous, and will shine out in a shady area of the garden. Foxgloves are biennial and will self-seed easily. I actually do some in seed trays each year to ensure a ready supply, and they are easy to transplant if you find a seedling in the 'wrong' place. Make sure that you leave some flower heads so that they seed around the garden. There are other types of foxglove, but the common

Left Cottage pinks have delicate grey–green foliage, a strong scent and exquisite flowers

Below, top This is an unnamed rose that I inherited; its renewed vigour is a result of lots of mulching and a good spring pruning

Below, bottom *Allium* 'Purple Sensation'

Digitalis purpurea is the best known and most distinctively 'cottage'.

In early summer the roses are in flower, and some will keep going until early autumn or even longer. Romantic, beautiful and often fragrant, roses may be shrubs, climbers, ramblers, hybrid tea bushes, miniatures, antique or modern, floribundas or species; some grow to incredible heights by scrambling up trees, while others work well in a pot. There are thousands of varieties; some will repeat flower, others are disease resistant, and there are even thornless roses. I have planted them as structure in the border with companion plants around them. They do need some care and attention and can be prone to various problems, but the roses I got from David Austin have been disease-free; I have 'Gabriel Oak' in the centre of the bed and 'Claire Austin' climbing over metal arches that I installed along the path.

Beneath the roses and through the borders in early summer I have *Allium* 'Purple Sensation', which is a medium-height bulb. It's so easy and reliable to grow; it smells sweet and has wonderful globe-shaped seed heads which add structure right through until late autumn. After that the stems start to break and fall apart but they can be easily dried and bought indoors: a welcome reminder of their past glories. There are many different alliums (including various onions that you'd find in the vegetable patch), and some have absolutely enormous flower heads with individual star-shaped flowers. I grow a little bright yellow *Allium moly* at the base of some deep purple aeonium – quite a striking combination.

Ephemerals

Sweet rocket (*Hesperis matronalis*) is a very attractive biennial that is fragrant, especially in the evening. It's a bit similar to honesty (*Lunaria annua*) and self-seeds, so you tend to find it repeating itself throughout a cottage garden. It is usually pink or white, and known for attracting bees, butterflies and other beneficial insects.

Larkspurs and delphiniums are tall plants with attractive flowers that are excellent for cutting. They need staking and are a little susceptible to slugs and snails, but really make a show-stopping centrepiece. Delphiniums are perennial plants, and larkspurs are annuals. Both come in shades of blue, pink, red, white and purple, and like a free-draining soil in a sunny and sheltered site. I grow the annual 'giant' larkspur (*Consolida ajacis*), which self-seeds so easily that I have to carefully edit out many of the seedlings.

Sweet peas need something to climb up, and a bamboo wigwam covered in a riot of pink, purple, white and red flowers is quintessentially 'cottage garden'. They smell wonderful and last well in a vase indoors, and at traditional village flower and produce shows the competition for best sweet pea is fierce. There are many tricks when growing from seed, including scratching the seed or soaking in water overnight before sowing, but basically they are sown in winter and kept in a frost-free environment before planting out in spring. (Alternatively, if overwintering young plants is difficult, you can sow in spring for a slightly later display.) Tie them into a structure to grow over and make sure that you deadhead the flowers to keep the show going.

Above Sweet rocket **(left)** and larkspur **(right)** are perfect summer companions

Long-lasting hardy geraniums

Geraniums come in many forms, are perennial and hardy (and not to be confused with pelargoniums, a tender perennial which is often called a geranium). They may be pink, white, blue, or anything in between, and though there are early spring versions, most flower in summer. If you cut them back hard in midsummer, it's amazing how fast the foliage will regrow and you may well enjoy a second flush of

Above *Geranium macrorrhizum* (left) and sweet peas (right)

flowers. The cutting back can benefit the neighbouring plants, too, as the foliage can get floppy and fall across other plants, hiding them. Geraniums are an excellent groundcover plant and will spread to fill gaps. If they spread too much, the ones at the edges can be pulled out and replanted elsewhere.

Wildlife favourites

Umbellifers form a much-loved part of the cottage garden and come into their own in early to midsummer. There are many wild species (cow parsley, wild carrot, hogweed and pignut, for example), but in domestic gardens we tend to avoid these as they can be invasive; they have a prodigious number of seeds and some species are also poisonous. Umbellifers have umbrella-shaped flower heads which attract insects, so they are fabulous plants for a wildlife-friendly garden, and there are many that we use as herbs in the kitchen (dill and fennel come to mind). Angelica is a good example of a cottage garden plant with culinary use, attractive to insects, and very beautiful as a statement plant. It is biennial and can be easily raised from seed. I grow bishop's flower (*Ammi majus*), which has large and impressive heads of delicate flowers that are excellent for cutting.

Every year I look forward to seeing what I like to call 'our' hummingbird hawk-moths; in spring and early summer these amazing little moths fly from the Continent and turn up all over the UK, but mostly in southern counties. One of the plants that they love is valerian (*Centranthus ruber*). This plant may be red, pink or white, and looks lovely when growing in or on top of walls. Be careful, though, as its roots can damage stonework, and it seeds prolifically.

Lady's mantle (*Alchemilla mollis*) is a soft-leaved perennial with a mass of frothy yellow-green flowers. Its leaves collect the dewdrops or rain, it grows in crevices or between paving stones, and it is a popular flower for a vase or in an arrangement. Easy from seed or by division, it requires little care and is an ideal 'companion' plant, giving a soft green backdrop and covering the ground profusely if left to spread. In late summer, when the flowers are spent and the plant becomes untidy, cut it back and it will form new and fresh-looking foliage. (This also helps to prevent a forest of seedlings.)

Honeysuckle (*Lonicera periclymenum*) is a cottage garden climber that is native to the UK. It belongs to a family that also contains shrubs that can be grown into topiary or hedging, but the climbing

Below, left Dill is a useful herb in the kitchen, and also a striking-looking plant

Below, right Valerian (*Centranthus ruber*) is very attractive to moths and bees

Right This honeysuckle in a Somerset garden is growing up through an old garden bench

'woodbine', as it was known, is fragrant and attractive to bees and the most familiar garden variety. It has berries in autumn which the birds love (they're poisonous to humans), and it smells lovely. Its tubular flowers are usually yellow, white or pink, and keep going until autumn. Make sure the soil around the plant is moist, and feed occasionally in spring. It goes especially well with roses.

Right, clockwise from top left *Papaver somniferum* (opium poppy), *Papaver rhoeas* (field poppy), *Papaver nudicaule* (Iceland poppy) and *Papaver somniferum* 'Danish Flag'

Glorious poppies

We can't discuss the cottage garden in early summer without mention of the poppy family. There are many species, from the humble but iconic annual field poppy (*Papaver rhoeas*) that grows in disturbed ground and is a potent symbol of the First World War – and all the soldiers who died – to the stately and exuberant oriental poppy (*Papaver orientale*), which is perennial and usually pink, red or white. There are also opium poppies, Iceland poppies, California poppies, Welsh poppies and even Himalayan poppies. Opium poppy (*Papaver somniferum*) is a tall annual that has some beautiful colourings (I have 'Danish Flag', which is a rather crazy fringed version with red and white petals), and perennial Welsh poppies (*Papaver cambricum*) turn up everywhere in spring and right through the summer, seeding themselves freely.

What to do in the early summer garden

Early summer is an exciting time in the gardener's calendar. It seems that the whole garden is pushing upwards and outwards, with fresh green growth and vibrant colour everywhere. In spring the plants that had survived the winter in the border were jostling for position with new plants just arrived from the greenhouse or windowsill. Now the same plants are fighting for space in your packed cottage garden border. Watch out for casualties, though – you may suddenly find that a treasured little specimen, carefully placed in prime position, has been crowded out and is possibly lying dormant – or worse, dead – beneath a much more accomplished bully of a plant. So, keep an eye on all this growth; stake those that are growing quickly, and place plant supports around those that threaten to shoot up; it's better to do it now rather than later, when the plant has grown too fast and you are reduced to desperately trying to support an over-large and unwieldy titan!

Tulips can be lifted from pots once their foliage has died down, and stored for autumn planting, and the containers that they were

in freed up for another display. When digging up the bulbs, clean off any rotten or loose skin, chop off the foliage and leave to dry out for a few days. Then place in a ventilated container in a dry and cool place until autumn. Some people store them in sacking or old produce nets. Tulips in the garden often don't grow as well after the first year, so I like to take the ones that have been used in pots and plant them at the edge of borders so they can be easily reached when ready to be picked for a vase next year.

Keeping the 'weeds' under control is always top of a gardener's list of jobs, and at this time of year it's particularly important. However much you think you're in charge, they seem to appear behind your back and are 15 cm/6 inches high before you know it. As we know, a cottage garden is an informal and edited collection of plants that relies as much on happenstance as on careful design, so it's important to allow some 'weeds' to grow. There is a lovely stand of teasels beneath the bird box in my garden, and it was lucky that as a wildflower enthusiast I had recognized the young seedlings as they grew (they have a distinctive white stripe down the middle of the leaves), so these were allowed to stay. However, there are definitely plants that I don't want crowding out the

Above The garden needs to be cleared of some of the forget-me-nots (*Myosotis sylvatica*), and I am hoeing through the borders trying to keep down excess seedlings

Above Dahlia plants that have been brought on in the potting shed and acclimatized to the conditions outside, ready for planting

cottage classics, and a good session with the hoe is both useful and strangely meditative.

As you look around the early summer borders, you'll probably see gaps appearing. At the moment, my forget-me-nots, which did well this year, are over, and I am pulling out vast sprawling patches of them. The gaps are quite obvious, even though they tend to clamber up and through the tiniest of spaces, so it's good to plan ahead to have something for later. I want the garden to be a continuous show of colour and interest, so 'successional' planting is important. The dahlias that I saved last year and kept stored in a cardboard box in the potting shed have been replanted in pots under cover and are ready for their moment. I have given them a week or two in the cold frame outside and can now put them in the gaps. In traditional cottage gardens, the dahlias would often be planted in the vegetable patch, usually in a line. They were grown to cut for vases indoors or for the village show, and they benefited from the well-prepared, rich soil of the veg patch. However, I don't really have room for that, so I use the dahlias as gap-fillers; they grow quickly, some are quite tall, and they give great colour right through until autumn. Watch out for the slugs and snails (a forage with a torch on a damp night will yield a huge number), and stake them, as they have rather brittle stems.

Another way to fill gaps is use pots that have been planted with tall bulbs like lilies. These can be moved around, and as they are tall rather than wide, they can be slipped into smaller gaps with instant effect. Other gap-fillers are annuals such as poppies that will grow quickly and provide colour right through until autumn. Scatter the seed as and when you see a space.

As already mentioned, the roses are of course looking lovely in early summer, but there are still jobs to be done with them. You can tie in any long shoots of climbers and ramblers horizontally as they get established, as this encourages flowering the following year. There is also deadheading to do, and again this encourages more

flowers. The plant's primary focus is to produce flowers, and as a result seed heads, so if you cut off the dead heads before they set seed, the plant will try again to flower. Deadheading is also a calming and enjoyable job, and it gives you the chance to take a look at the garden; you will undoubtedly spot further jobs, but, all the same, I find it very relaxing.

Above One of gardening's most satisfying jobs: deadheading

Cottage containers in early summer

The arrival of summer suddenly brings with it the longer days, the warmer weather (we hope!), and a profusion of new flowering and foliage plants that can be used in containers. The cottage garden 'feel' can be brought into your patio or courtyard, around the back door, or on to the city balcony and window box. The planting should be informal, mixed and perhaps even a little eccentric. Think recycled pots and containers of all types, plants dug out of the garden, vegetables or herbs and even garden gnomes.

The selection of plants available to buy at this time of year is, of course, huge, but don't forget to hold back some plants that you have grown from seed for the border.

A ROUND-UP OF
EARLY SUMMER JOBS

1 Lift and store tulip bulbs after flowering.

2 Support tall-growing perennials, including hollyhocks and delphiniums, with a sturdy cane.

3 Tie in new stems of climbing and rambling roses horizontally to supports in order to encourage more flowers next year.

4 Fill any gaps in borders with pots of tall bulbs, such as fragrant lilies, to add instant colour.

5 Spread mulch around thirsty crops such as beans and courgettes to hold in moisture around their roots.

6 Apply tomato feed regularly to fruiting veg crops, including tomatoes.

7 Plant out dahlia tubers and cannas after all risk of frost has passed.

8 Continue sowing annuals, such as California poppies, into gaps in borders for colour from midsummer into autumn.

9 Plant out summer bedding and tender annuals, including sunflowers, cosmos and nasturtiums, after the last frost.

10 Reduce snail populations by going on regular evening hunts, especially during damp weather.

A PROJECT FOR AN EARLY SUMMER DAY

Planting out snapdragons and other tender seedlings

(clockwise from top left)

Clear an area ready for the plants and dig a big enough hole

Position the small plant

Water the plant in

Firm the soil around the plant

Left Cottage garden summer
containers, with *Achillea*
'Walther Funcke' surrounded
by calibrachoas in small
terracotta pots

Below I find that small
collections of containers
often work best. It's easy to
swap them around and make
different arrangements,
perhaps as plants go over or
new ones are ready

local garage) and a reed canary grass (*Phalaris arundinacea*) that I
had transplanted in the garden, they made a lovely show in an old
tin tub that I was reusing. Mix the plants, cottage style, but keep in
mind what the overall effect will be. Aim for a mix of heights but try
to arrange them so that you actually see the different elements; for
example, in this case the grass works best at the back. And although
colours in a cottage garden are generally quite a jumble, with a
smaller space the effect is more obvious, so keep in mind some sort
of colour scheme.

The types of plant we can use in containers are many too. There
are annual bedding type plants that work well and these are usually
tender species that flower profusely for one season and are great in
pots or as gap-fillers in borders. Calibrachoa (also known as million
bells) is a good example: it comes in a range of colours, including
lavender, blue, pink, red, magenta, yellow, orange, coral and white.

A trailing plant, it looks best spilling over the edges of window
boxes, pots and hanging baskets. Best of all, in my view, is that it
is much beloved by moths. There is a strong argument that annual
bedding plants aren't good for the environment. They are usually

grown for sale in huge greenhouses, often supplied in plastic pots, and many are of no use to pollinating insects. They also need a lot of watering and artificial fertilizers to keep them flowering throughout summer. So, if you can grow your own bedding from seed, that would be a huge help, and it's also the way that the original cottage gardeners would have gone about things. Sow seeds in mid-spring on a windowsill or in the greenhouse, and slowly acclimatize once they have germinated and been pricked out. And, while discussing ways of growing annuals in a more environmentally friendly way, when watering pots use your water butt and try making your own fertilizer. A simple mix can be made with borage and a bucket of water. Stuff the bucket about half-full with roughly chopped leaves, stems and flowers of borage. Pack them in tightly, then fill with water. You can use tap-water or water from a rain barrel, or speed the process by using hot (but not boiling) water. Set aside to soak for a day in the sun and cover with fine mesh to prevent insects from laying eggs. Strain out the borage leaves and fill up a watering can with the mixture. Pour it on the soil or spray the leaves of your plants as a foliar feed. The plants should show an improvement very quickly.

Above This collection of early summer containers in Julie Quinn's London garden makes great use of grasses, which will keep going for much of the year

Above, left An old wooden barrel water butt makes a pleasing centrepiece

Above, right A large terracotta pot of diascia will keep going for months in this collection of cottage garden containers

Then there are the perennials, either tender (types of fuchsia, for example), which would need to be overwintered in a greenhouse or similar, or hardy (an old favourite, *Erysimum* 'Bowles's Mauve', is a good choice), and these can, of course, be planted out in the border after use in containers. Perennials, if planted on their own in a simple clay pot, can be so useful. Not only do they make excellent individual potted plants, but they can easily be moved around to pair with other plants in a display, or popped into the border to fill any gaps. Don't forget that in a pot they will need regular watering and possibly require feeding. And even repotting after a couple of years. As they are long-lived, they will need regular deadheading to keep the flowers going. There really are so many different perennials to choose from, but it's good to go for plants that the bees and other insects love: salvias are a good choice and will keep flowering until the first frosts. That cottage garden favourite valerian (*Centranthus ruber*), in either red or white, is irresistible to the hummingbird hawk-moths which we are lucky enough to have in our garden during summer.

There are also plenty of early summer bulbs that look good in pots, and the smaller agapanthus are a winner, along with lilies

and gladioli. As ever with bulbs, we need to think ahead, and these should either be left in the pot and bought out to display just in time, or planted each year, usually three months before.

The choice of pot to use is yours, but the cottage garden style would be to reuse and recycle. I have just put some London pride (*Saxifraga* × *urbium*) in a kitchen colander which had broken, and the effect is rather lovely. It's the right shape for the plant, and the airy flowers that appear in late spring and early summer are pure 'cottage'. I have a collection of tin buckets and many old terracotta pots to choose from, and my advice would be to keep an eye on the local ad pages of your social media to try and buy up affordable bits and pieces. And don't throw anything away!

Inspiring early summer gardens

Early summer is such an intensely beautiful time in most gardens, but especially so in the cottage garden. The colour combinations, and even clashes, are riveting, the speed of growth is amazing, and the way that nature seems to fill every gap is fascinating. So much so that I can't really pick just one inspiring garden in this section. I have chosen the truly groundbreaking Gravetye Manor in Sussex,

Above, left Waste not, want not: a broken kitchen colander makes an interesting container for London pride (*Saxifraga* × urbium)

Above, right Helen Grimes's seaside cottage garden in Devon in its full glory

Above, left and right Piers Newth and Louise Allen have created this gorgeous and authentic cottage garden in Oxfordshire

where Tom Coward and his team garden on a large scale while always keeping in mind the type of cottage garden planting its creator, William Robinson, became famed for; and at the other end of the scale, Helen Grimes's Old Stone Cottage at Beesands in south Devon, on a coastal site with views across the road to the beach, is a perfect cottage garden packed with flowers: sweet peas, clematis, larkspurs and cosmos are jammed together in this fragrant and colourful space, with dahlias and agapanthus promising colour for many weeks to come. Also, there is Julia Thyer's garden, Fernbank, in Somerset, a pot-crammed plot near Bristol, with vignettes, vistas and secret corners. And then there is the garden of Piers Newth and Louise Allen in Oxfordshire, immaculately kept and filled with gardening paraphernalia gleaned from far and wide; and Louisa Morgan's atmospheric garden in Wales.

It's a bit of a mixture, but I hope you can see that the overriding theme is consistent. These gardens tend to have a fairly simple layout with features which are often rustic. The planting is informal and jam-packed, using simple flowers that attract insects. Plants are a mixture of heights and shapes and there are many self-seeders; they scramble over walls and through each other, and there seems to be no bare soil. The space is well used, and part of the romance of the cottage garden is that it's often difficult to see where you are; there are hidden areas, bits you can't see and surprises around every corner. These are gardens for wildlife, gardens for cutting flowers and, above all, gardens to lift the spirit. Not easy maintenance, these are time-consuming and thoughtful gardens that are productive and seasonal. Gardens for the soul, in fact.

What and how to photograph in early summer

Well, where to start? Early summer is bonanza time for a photographer in the garden. Suddenly there is a lot of colour; the bulbs are well and truly flowering their socks off, and there are myriad other plants that are enjoying the warmth of the sun. Roses have started to bloom, there are sweetly scented shrubs, and annuals abound. As the sun has now climbed higher in the sky and its strength is really kicking in, it is important to think about the light when it comes to your photography. There are no shortcuts, and it's time to set your alarm clock. The early morning and perhaps late evening are the times of day to get out and take pictures. The so-called 'golden hour' is when the sun is low enough in the sky to give soft and directional lighting. Textures are picked out by this soft and angled light; there is less contrast and there's a warmth to the light. Don't forget to check the aspect of the garden, though; there is nothing worse than getting up at the crack of dawn, missing breakfast and lugging your tripod and camera bag into the garden, only to find that the garden is west-facing and doesn't get decent sun until the evening. Or that the resident oak tree shields the garden until halfway through the morning. However, if all goes well, there's nothing like catching the sun as it rises behind a magnificent border, picking out the edges of the flowers with a soft glow. It's also good to remember that the early mornings are often still; many a great picture has been ruined by a plant that just won't stay put!

Obviously, you can photograph at any time of the day, but to get a real cracker you will need decent light. Sometimes it is possible to shoot later in the day in summer, but the conditions need to be favourable. A very light cloud cover can work, and the softness this gives can work well with plant portraits, for example, but if you are after the sweeping panoramas with a wow factor, then photograph at either end of the day when the sun is nearer to the

Above, top and middle Early summer at Gravetye Manor

Above, bottom Glorious wisteria in Julia Thyer's Somerset garden

Above The garden of Louisa Morgan in Wales, shot as the sun is going down

horizon. I would always suggest using a tripod if possible – the obvious reason being that the camera doesn't shake when taking the exposure – but I also think that it slows you down (in a good way) and makes you compose more thoughtfully. I do hand-hold the camera sometimes too, and with modern lenses that have inbuilt 'shake reduction' features, this is perfectly possible. And it enables you to get into more tricky positions and work more quickly. But, as a rule, use a tripod; it's one of your most important pieces of equipment. Lastly, if using a mobile phone, the advice about the early sunlight still applies, but do watch out for lens flare. Mobile phone cameras generally don't have lens hoods, and so flare can be a problem; it can look quite atmospheric, but usually it just degrades the image and reduces contrast. Use your hand to block off the sunlight coming in at an angle to the phone and bouncing off; this is what causes flare.

FEATURES AND FOCAL POINTS

The early cottage gardeners, with their history of make-do-and-mend and loathing of waste, used anything to hand to make their gardens pretty. A broken teapot might house a little herb, and a bucket that had seen better days could be planted up with bulbs found in the border or some prized cuttings from a friend's much-admired pinks. Arches might be made from rustic repurposed wood, and an old cider barrel could be reused as a water butt for the vegetable patch. The very structure of the garden would be part of the charm: a white-painted picket fence or an old stone wall covered with ivy or honeysuckle being as much part of the cottage garden 'look' as a border filled to overflowing with columbines and forget-me-nots. And the path that traverses this plant-filled paradise is just as important as the walls that delineate the bounds of the garden.

So, let's take a look at some of these features and how you can incorporate them into your own garden.

Paths

It seems obvious, but usually the best path is the one that goes where you want to go in the quickest way. So, a straight path from front gate to front door, for example. In my own garden, I was also careful to make sure the paths were a generous width, wide enough for a wheelbarrow, and wide enough to allow plants to spill across paths.

Traditionally, the likelihood is that the path would have been of beaten earth, or perhaps a cobbling together of paving or discarded stones. Nowadays we have a much greater choice,

but those traditional finishes both work well and are reasonably priced. I left grass paths, with stepping stones that we found around the garden, in areas that get a lot of traffic. Gravel is a good easy-to-use and easy-to-maintain alternative, but will usually require some edging to prevent the gravel spilling into the borders. Again, the choice of edge should be suitably rustic and in a cottage style, with plants that spill on to the path softening the look. A herringbone brick path has a soft-edged and romantic look but is practical too, and if you can find some old bricks that have been

materials and styles. Recycling and reusing were all part of the cottager's life, and very little went to waste. If you are lucky, a good rummage around your local vintage or antique shop can bring you a prize piece (remember, though, that, however rustically charming a chair looks, it needs to be solid enough to be sat on.)

There's nothing quite like a well-earned drink in the garden at the end of a busy day, whether it's at a table or perhaps at a carefully situated bench. Benches were often placed near the front door and would have been simple, with two strong wooden uprights and a plank across the top – or, in areas where stone was plentiful, this would have been used. Whatever you choose for your own garden, a year or two of weathering helps blend it in, and the growth of surrounding plants completes the look. Wooden tables suit a cottage garden; a friend of ours made a lovely and very rustic table from an old door (complete with hinges and locks) to sit on our 'patio' area.

saved from the scrap heap, then all the better. Again, plants growing between the bricks help soften the look, so leave soil rather than laying cement in between. Steps should be simple and rustic-looking. Stone or wood (perhaps railway sleepers) can be used, but remember that they should be stable, and constructed properly. (Nothing worse than wobbly footing!)

Arches, pergolas and plant supports

An arch or pergola smothered with roses or honeysuckle is a typical cottage garden feature, and makes a perfect focal point. An arch, especially built across a pathway, lends height and scale to the garden, and also leads the eye through the borders on either side. Obviously, as they will stay outside all year round, arches and pergolas need to be sturdy and weather-resistant; so, if they are wooden, it's sensible to use a preservative on the wood. A painted finish can be pleasing, but this will need regular maintenance. Plant supports can often be moved at the end of the season (if supporting annuals, for instance), but again, if not, do ensure they are up to facing the weather, and securely fixed into the ground. One of the main plant supports in my own garden is a simple lashed-together set of hazel branches cut from a neighbour's field,

Furniture

Part of the charm of the cottage garden lies in the somewhat random mixture of bits and pieces of furniture of different vintages,

Left Caervallack Garden in Cornwall, at midsummer: an arch leads the eye through to an old garden roller and to the cob wall beyond

Above A garden at Prawle Point in South Devon, with a set of railway sleeper steps

Right The traditional cottage garden grass path at Bowhay House

Below In Annie Stanford's Somerset garden, encroaching plants colonize an old wooden bench

pleasingly bent and rough, and these have now lasted two years through sun and rain. I also have some rather elegant rusted metal supports that are a very simple obelisk shape, and they give shape and structure to the borders.

Ornament

I remember visiting East Lambrook Garden to take photographs many years ago and seeing a slightly crumbling sundial surrounded and overgrown by geraniums. The photograph I took that day has been published many times to illustrate 'the cottage garden style'. A simple birdbath, placed at the centre of a border, or perhaps at the end of a path as a focal point, also makes a lovely picture. Stone ornaments, once weathered in, can look as if they have been there forever.

Old tin watering cans, or tin tubs, overflowing with trailing plants provide a nice touch. I have also used an old water tank from the loft as a giant plant container – or how about planting up an old and conveniently holey wheelbarrow? Lovely old containers, whether they are secondhand terracotta pots rescued from the local tip, holey tin buckets, broken teapots or even disused colanders, look the part. Broken garden tools can be reused as ornaments too. My shed has a rusty fork attached to it, and three ancient metal garden sieves that the honeysuckle is now colonizing. Among the many things I found while digging the borders were horseshoes, which have now been nailed to the shed door. (This was commonly done by the old cottagers, for luck.)

Gates and doors

We all know the function of a gate or door, but beyond being the obvious entrance or exit from a garden, a gate or a half-opened door can lead you in visually, offering a tempting glimpse of what lies beyond. It's a commonly used photographic technique to fill the frame of the picture with the half-open door, the garden beyond enticing you to enter. Cottage gates should be suitably rustic and probably made of wood, although a simple rusted metal gate has its charm as well. And, of course, an arch, perhaps made of wood and covered with a climber, can be built over the gate; or even, if the gate is in a gap in the hedge, one can allow the hedge to grow across and over the gate.

Cottage doors are usually simple wooden plank affairs, often painted – and the frame would frequently have been enhanced with a climber.

Above, left The rustic table (once a door) on a brick patio at Bowhay House

Above, middle At Bullock Horn Cottage in Wiltshire, a pergola shades elegant garden furniture

Above, right A sundial makes a lovely centrepiece

Roses and honeysuckles are good choices, and both of these have a soft and informal appeal, and the added benefit of scent. Especially if you have a bench at the front door, it's a cottage tradition to plant scented plants – perhaps stocks, lavender or tobacco plants – beside it. This provides a fragrant moment to savour the garden ahead – or, indeed, the garden behind.

Patios and courtyards

When we moved into our cottage, there was a rather neglected corner of the garden that had a raised bed with a selection of leftovers from the previous inhabitants' attempts at a vegetable garden. It soon became obvious that the spot had been picked because it caught a lot of afternoon sun, and (giving ourselves priority over the vegetables) we decided to turn it into a little courtyard or patio to sit in and relax of an afternoon. So, using some old discarded bricks rescued from a friend who had dismantled a chimney, I made a paved courtyard which is now home to the rustic table made from an old farmyard door. As with all building projects. it's important to do the proper preparation, in this case, levelling the land and putting down a weedproof membrane, before using a sand layer

to bed the bricks on. (If you are unsure about how to do something properly, get an expert in – it will save you in the long run – or at least check out the 'how-to' videos online.)

When deciding on which materials to use, remember what the cottagers would have done: recycle and reuse! Sustainability is important, and apart from being better for the planet, it looks so much more in keeping with a traditional cottage garden. I used sand between the bricks because it is permeable and allows the water to escape (important if you are in an area prone to flooding), and it also allows plants to grow between, which again is better for nature and softens the look of the surface. You can actually introduce some plants too: lady's mantle, thyme, fleabane, chamomile and some of the small succulents would all do well and look fabulous. (Keep on top of weeding, though, as some plants take a hold in sand and then grow like crazy as soon as you turn your back!) And I find that an application of fine sand once a year keeps the surface looking fresh.

Boundaries

Every garden has a boundary, and whether it be hedge, fence or wall, a boundary is as important a part of the garden as the middle. Often, the boundaries are an opportunity to use climbers and give height (and scent, perhaps) to the garden. The sort of cheap-looking treated wooden fences that you buy in large DIY stores tend to look out of place in a cottage garden, but if they are covered with climbers, or at least painted, this will help soften the effect. Natural materials are always best in a cottage garden, and a woven willow fence, for example, can look a picture even if it's not covered with climbers. A white-painted picket fence is a classic cottage garden look.

Low willow hurdles can provide a boundary to borders too, and the process of actually weaving them yourself is not only quite simple, but satisfying as well. I have a friend with a willow patch and he was only too pleased for me to come and get rid of his cuttings; an afternoon's work weaving them between hazel poles to make a

Above, left Ivy covering a stone sphere

Above, middle A garden gate in Somerset

Above, right A view through a gateway into Vanessa Berridge's Gloucestershire garden

Left A paved circular patio at Bramble Torre in Devon

Below A reflection of laundry on a woven willow fence at Bowhay House

curved edge for the border was well worth it for both of us.

Stone walls are a traditional boundary in the cottage garden, and we have one on one side of our patch. It's covered with ivy, and as long as the ivy doesn't start creeping across the border, I am relaxed about any pruning or cutting back. Ivy is a hugely valuable source of pollen for many bees and butterflies during the autumn and winter, and it also has a softening effect. The stones have obviously been there for some time (probably hundreds of years) and are covered with lichens and pennyworts.

A hedge can obviously take a while to grow to size, but if you are lucky enough to have one already, treasure it. Here in Devon, by the sea, the favourite hedging plant is griselinia, an evergreen and salt-tolerant shrub that grows quickly and has lovely soft green foliage. I have shaped mine to echo the hills beyond, and the abundant foliage is an ideal nesting site for many blackbirds, robins and wrens. A good boundary can create a microclimate; the griselinia has a border in front which is significantly drier and more sheltered than the rest of the garden. Always remember when trimming a hedge not to do it during the nesting season for birds. Hedges are a wildlife haven, much more so than a fence, even one covered with climbers. (Always look after the occupants!)

Through the seasons

LATE SUMMER IN THE COTTAGE GARDEN

Globe thistle (*Echinops ritro* 'Veitch's Blue') and montbretia (*Crocosmia* 'Fire King') add warmth to the colours of late summer at Bowhay House

A snapshot of late summer at Bowhay House

Late summer has waded in (literally, it seems, as this July was the wettest on record) and the garden has flopped a little and become a bit 'blowsy'. There is a tall hollyhock that has survived the high winds thanks to a scaffold of bamboo that surrounds it. Much of the early summer colour has been yanked out; I left foxglove spikes until they were well dried out and a deep brown so that the seeds were scattered across the borders, and the sweet william has been cut right back. Soldiering on, though, are the cornflowers with their unfeasibly blue flowers; I sowed these and grew them on the windowsill in early spring (I think they are *Centaurea cyanus* 'Blue Ball'), and they serve as testament to what can be grown from a cheap packet of seed in just one year. They are almost 1.5 metres/5 feet tall and have been in flower for months. The bees and hoverflies are mad for them, and the goldfinches have been teaching their young how to pick apart the seed heads for food. I have deadheaded most of them until recently, which keeps the show going, but I am now letting them all go to seed so that I will have a supply for next year. Now is, in fact, a good time to sow annual seeds, so I will soon be able to get some new plants going, ready for the spring.

The dahlias are growing well, although the snails, which have reappeared after a dry June, have somewhat denuded them of flowers. My daisies (*Leucanthemum* 'Edgeworth Giant') are the size of saucers this year and work well as a kind of rhythmic structure. I have planted a few of them at regular intervals through the borders, and even though they can get battered and floppy in bad weather, if kept in order they are fabulous long-term flowerers. Also doing very well are hollyhocks (*Alcea rosea*), one of which is rising a good 2.5 metres/8 feet above the border, giving height and flamboyance to the early morning view from the bedroom window.

The miniscule vegetable patch has supplied a good crop of broad beans, even though we only planted a handful, and once these had

finished, I cut the plants at the base and left the roots in place. Like other legumes, broad beans have bacteria in the nodules on their roots which 'fix' nitrogen in the soil and so boost the level of this important soil nutrient. I have planted some dill now in their place, and as well as being a tasty herb if scattered in a salad and excellent with fish, this umbellifer is a real insect magnet. Another umbellifer I planted earlier in the season was *Visnaga daucoides* 'Green Mist', formerly known as *Ammi visnaga*, not to eat but to cut for a vase. It's also beloved by insects and its frothy green foliage does look like a 'green mist'.

The tomatoes I have grown from seed ('Tigerella') are ripening well now, with four or five bunches per plant. Unfortunately, there is some fruit 'splitting', which is a result of uneven watering due to the excessive rain. They still taste good (although I think the ubiquitous 'Gardener's Delight' that I grew last year had a better flavour), and I will keep an eagle eye out for the dreaded blight which can affect tomatoes in a wet year. (Postscript: writing this at the end of August, I have to report that the blight did indeed strike, and there will now be an excess of green tomato chutney!)

All gardeners know that the year-on-year, season-by-season process of making a garden is a gathering of not just seeds and

Above The sunflowers **(left)** and dahlias **(right)** have fared well, and the bees have had a field day

plants, but of learned experience and wisdom. So, for instance, I know that even in this tiny patch, there are areas that are drier, shadier, damper or sunnier. Some areas where the soil is better and some where the wind whistles through more forcefully. The stone wall that dries the soil on one side or the shade made by the house, and even the wavy hedge that protects from wind, are all factors to consider. There's also my favourite tree, a lovely ancient hawthorn, that is a wildlife haven but dries the soil beneath. In this shady border down the side of the garden, Japanese anemones (*Anemone × hybrida*) grow well, but I have noticed that the last two years' flowering has been rather poor. I suspect that it's because the roots have become too congested, so I have decided to replant the whole area. I will dig up some of it in late autumn in order to thin it out, and then add a good mulch. There are also a small cherry tree (perhaps *Prunus* 'Kursar', but I can't be totally sure) and an old hydrangea. Both seem to thrive in this border. And woven through beneath these two is a host of hellebores that will come into their own during winter and early spring.

As this long summer has progressed, I have picked out certain sections of the garden that have needed a little editing. The self-seeders have, on the whole, done well, but in my desire to fill gaps I have definitely made some errors. Some of the dahlias that I planted in early summer stick out like sore thumbs. They are, by their nature, big and showy eye-catchers, and my main mistake was not labelling them with their colours last year when I took them out of the ground. So, while a cottage garden is usually a riot of colour and shapes, the orange-bronze dahlia that squats alongside a stately pink meadowsweet (*Filipendula rubra* 'Venusta') looks distinctly wrong. Come October, I will pull the offenders out, label them, and store them for next year. Late summer is the time of year when all these mistakes are more obvious. The garden is no longer stitched together with the drifts of pink foxgloves or the vertical accents of the alliums. The planting can look disjointed and gaps appear, so that plants that sit together are

Above The extraordinary height of this hollyhock provides a perfect vertical accent to the late summer border. Cornflowers, larkspurs and daisies are the support act

more obvious in their differences and can clash more. I am already planning for next year and will make notes now to avoid some of these clashes. Having said all of this, none other than one of this country's greatest-ever 'colourful' gardeners, Christopher Lloyd, said, 'If you love colour, then try some outlandish combinations to see how you get on with them. Orange with magenta, for instance. I think those two work splendidly next to one another.' Be bold!

One of the joys of container planting is that mature plants in pots can be carefully positioned to fill the holes that appear in late summer, ironing out and repairing some of the broken 'weave' of the border. I used a pot of *Achillea* 'Walther Funcke' with its fabulous deep orange flowers to fill a gap where foxgloves had been, and I liked it so much I decanted it into the border. Next year (there's always next year), I think it will fill out and make a nice contrast with the ever-present blue love-in-a-mist (*Nigella damascena*) that self-seeds all over the garden.

Late summer is a time to spot and encourage (or indeed edit out) any seedlings that appear. Get your eye in and you will see so many, hiding beneath their parents' protective foliage, or seemingly miles away from the plants that supplied them. There is an annual here

Above, left *Visnaga daucoides* 'Green Mist' is a great cutting flower

Above, right The tiny tomato patch has produced a lot of fruit

Above Flamboyant flowering – the late summer garden can really sing with its riotous colour

that pops up all over called 'Fool's Parsley' (*Aethusa cynapium*), which is similar to edible parsley and a member of the umbellifer group of plants. Beware, it's poisonous, but it is very attractive to wildlife and really rather pretty: delicate with a bearded umbel and fine filigree foliage. I weed out a lot of it as it's so promiscuous, but I also leave quite a bit. It grows well beneath the aforementioned hawthorn. Another self-seeder which I have nursed this year is mullein (*Verbascum thapsus*), which produces fabulous spikes of impressive yellow flowers. It's a food for various insects, especially the mullein moth, which can decimate it, but it's worth leaving it and trying to remove the caterpillars by hand (easier before they get too large). As a biennial, it grows from seed in year one, then flowers in year two. I have transplanted some into small pots for a reserve supply, ready to plant early next year, but left most in the ground where they are. The caterpillars strike in late spring, so keep an eye out for them.

The stars of the cottage garden in late summer
Hollyhocks and more
Hollyhocks are perhaps one of the most picture-perfect and 'chocolate box' of all cottage garden plants. Mine have reached

2.5 metres/8 feet tall this year and, despite being affected by hollyhock rust (*Puccinia malvacearum*), they have flourished. They can be replaced every couple of years in order to reduce the effects of rust, and a clean border helps too. Pick up infected leaves or dig out badly affected whole plants and burn. I like the single flowers best, rather than the doubles (I planted some 'Chater's Double' this year, but they were affected by the rain we had in July and looked rather brown and soggy, I'm afraid). They love being against a wall, and as tall plants it suits them well. The deep reds are my favourites.

The daisies are a huge group of plants, so I can't go through them all here, but I am particularly keen on the leucanthemums, especially the long-lasting perennial types like our native ox-eye daisy (*Leucanthemum vulgare*) and Shasta daisy (*L. × superbum*). They are, like many daisies, white (or perhaps pale lemon), they have stiff stems, and they flower all summer. I have a big one called 'Edgeworth Giant' which is brilliant for giving structure to the border for a long period of time. It's big enough to be a backdrop to lots of other plants and the flower heads are as big as saucers. They are not fussy about soil, like a bit of sun and can be divided regularly (every couple of years). This gives you more plants for free.

I adore crocosmia, a flower which reminds me of the West Country, especially near the seaside. It has fiery funnel-shaped flowers in a range of colours and sword-shaped leaves, is easy to grow and can be carefully spread around the garden by digging up the corms (which look like flattened bulbs) and replanting them elsewhere. Some are invasive (watch out for *Crocosmia × crocosmiiflora*), so these should not be spread, but in general they make a lovely late summer and autumn show that gives warmth to the border. They look great against the blue of globe thistles (*Echinops ritro*).

Sun lovers (mostly)

Hylotelephium, otherwise known as sedum, is a succulent-leaved perennial with big flat flower heads in shades of red, pink and white. There are some with red leaves, too, and even some with variegated foliage. It is a real stalwart in the cottage garden, can be easily divided to create more plants, and the bees and butterflies flock to it. It likes full sun and won't really flower well in shade.

I am very fond of a combination of plants that is looking good at the moment against a willow fence. The tobacco plant *Nicotiana alata* and the so-called 'blackcurrant sage' (*Salvia microphylla* var. *microphylla*) work well together and form an airy mass of long-lasting

Right, clockwise from top left *Crocosmia* 'Star of the East'; *Hylotelephium* 'Sunset Cloud'; *Leucanthemum vulgare* 'Edgeworth Giant'; an unnamed red hollyhock (*Alcea rosea*)

flowers in red, green and white. The salvia is very easily propagated (take cuttings regularly), and I have a lot spread around. It may survive winter outdoors, but I keep pots indoors to bring out in spring. The nicotiana is best grown regularly from seed, but some people say that it can survive a year or two in the border if in a protected area. There is a lovely tobacco plant that grows quite tall but prefers dappled or part shade, *Nicotiana sylvestris*. It has white tubular flowers and can grow to a stately 1.5 metres/5 feet tall. Very much worth the effort if you have a shady border or woodland garden.

Gaura (*Oenothera lindheimeri*) is a long-flowering and floaty perennial that, a bit like the *Verbena bonariensis* it grows so well with, is tall and 'transparent'. The stems tend to flop at times and I sometimes need to support it, but it provides lovely late season colour and interest. It is easy to grow from seed or to propagate by cuttings, and it will flourish in most soils. Because of its floatiness it sometimes goes unnoticed, but it's good as a filler and weaves its long stems up through the plants that surround it. There is a well-known cultivar called 'Whirling Butterflies' that really 'does what it says on the tin': each flower looks like a miniature butterfly. Mostly white or pink.

Phlox is a group of plants that varies widely – from tiny rockery plants to tall, billowing cottage garden classics. The latter are what I am interested in, and a mound of healthy phlox in summer is a sight (and smell) to appreciate. They come in pink, red, white and blue, and can grow to a metre/39 inches tall. They are perennial, like moist soil but full sun and don't like to be crowded; leave space around them so that they don't get mildew. Otherwise, they are trouble-free and can easily form a fragrant 'backbone' to your cottage garden in summer.

Sunflowers have always been popular cottage garden annuals. They have big round faces and seem to be inherently happy plants. They are easy to grow from seed and are obviously impactful. Children love them and growing a sunflower from seed is an excellent way to introduce children to the delights of gardening. I prefer the slightly less 'giant' varieties and those with darker colours; 'Ruby Sunset' is a beauty, as is 'Velvet Queen'. Sunflowers give a vertical accent to the borders in late summer, so I position mine carefully. Keep the seeds when they have finished flowering, or leave them for the goldfinches.

What to do in the late summer garden

Late summer in the cottage garden can seem bittersweet; the healthy vigorous growth of early summer has abated and there may be visible gaps in the borders. As plants have finished flowering (forget-me-nots,

Below, top to bottom *Phlox paniculata* 'Franz Schubert'; *Helianthus* 'Velvet Queen'; *Oenothera lindheimeri* 'The Bride'

Above *Nicotiana mutabilis*

foxgloves and lupins, for example), they will have been cut hard back, ripped right out or left to seed. Whichever way, the gaps can be substantial or the resultant seedy stems untidy. Gap-filling with fast-growing late annuals, or even with containers of plants that can be moved around, helps, but there is definitely an element of nostalgia for those spectacular midsummer borders. Photographically speaking, it's tricky, but with careful positioning of the camera it's still possible to create lovely images; late summer is the season of warm reds, oranges and yellows, maybe a spider's web or two and dewdrops in the early morning. The hours are a bit easier too! First light is two hours later than it was at midsummer, so it's a veritable lie-in.

So, aside from clearing, tidying and staking, what else is to be done? There are seeds galore at this time, so get out the envelopes or paper bags and collect the seed bounty ready for next year. And if you have enough larkspurs, lupins or marigolds, then make sure that you chop off those seed heads and get rid of them before they disperse the seeds to all corners of the garden. Planning for next year may seem like you are wishing away a good part of this year, but an early sowing of foxgloves or sweet williams in a tray in the potting shed is good insurance against loss to the winter weather, and kicks off next year's show in style.

Staking and plant support are still important in late summer (though it's always best to stake before your plants flop over rather than after). My gauras, achilleas and dahlias have all been carefully staked, and this ensures that, instead of trailing across the path, they are providing height and punctuation in the garden. The plants are still growing, and with the lovely late sunshine we have had over the last few years, plants will keep growing well into mid- and even late autumn.

Those plants that need cutting back now (geraniums, for example) will have a regrowth of foliage and, in some cases, a second flush of flowers. They can be cut to ground level and the plant will quickly send up new leaves as long as the roots have some moisture.

Many shrubs can be pruned in summer once they have finished flowering. By doing this, you will reap the rewards of better displays. Pruning fruit trees or bushes will also help towards bigger crops. And even though my wisteria is young, I have cut back the long whippy new growth to about five leaves, to encourage flowering next year.

Late summer can be warm and watering well is vital, especially for potted plants. As the climate changes, watering can be a contentious subject, and in Devon we have had a hosepipe ban for much of this year. I use a couple of large old water butts that fill directly from the house gutters. A brief shower of rain can refill them, so I thoroughly recommend. We are also careful to use a washing-up bowl in the kitchen, and it really is a revelation when you add up the number of times it gets full. Take it outside, soap and all, and throw it around the border plants. A potted plant can need watering twice a day in very hot weather; do it either early or late in the day, so that precious water isn't wasted in evaporation as temperatures rise towards midday.

Above, left I am reusing this plastic water butt from the local tip, and trying to hide it behind a fuchsia bush

Above, right Cut back love-in-a-mist seed heads in late summer

A ROUND-UP OF
LATE SUMMER JOBS

1 Collect seeds from those plants that you want to keep, and get rid of those that you don't.

2 Sow hardy annual seeds and grow on in a cold frame or unheated greenhouse ready for next year.

3 Shear back chrysanthemums by as much as a third to encourage more flowers and growth.

4 Keep on picking cutting flowers for vases and they will keep flowering.

5 Support dahlias, lilies, gladioli and other soft-stemmed plants, as they are easily knocked around by the wind and rain.

6 Cut back geraniums to their base: they will look tidier and may even flower again.

7 Trim back lavender to just above any woody growth (you could even try drying the flowers, although fresh blooms dry best).

8 Prune wisteria to keep it in check and promote more flowering next year.

9 Sow a late batch of beetroot, spinach or radish; plenty of salad leaves will also grow quickly at this time of year.

10 Prune flowering shrubs once they are finished blooming; philadelphus, weigela and other summer-flowering shrubs can be pruned now.

A PROJECT FOR A LATE SUMMER DAY

Collecting seeds from garden angelica

(clockwise from top left)

Collect the seed head

Shake off the seeds

Name and date the packet

Store in a paper envelope

Left Lobelia × speciosa 'Hadspen Purple', aeoniums, dahlias, a small pittosporum and a large tin tub with grasses and achillea in this late summer container display

Left *Lobelia × speciosa* 'Hadspen Purple', aeoniums, dahlias, a small pittosporum and a large tin tub with grasses and achillea in this late summer container display

Below, left An unnamed pink dahlia mixes well with *Phlox paniculata* 'Goliath' and a tin bucket of purple heucheras and ferns

Below, right A group of *Persicaria* 'Red Dragon', *Phlox paniculata* 'Goliath', *Stipa arundinacea* and a large tin tub filled with dahlias in a corner of the garden

Cottage containers in late summer

As the garden slowly moves past its early summer glory, late summer containers can really fill the gaps and keep the show going for another month or so. At this time, colours in the garden tend to be at the hot end of the spectrum (early summer tends to be all pinks, blues and the paler colours, whereas late summer is reds, yellows and oranges), so there are a number of options for making up some bold and brilliant pots.

Dahlias come to mind immediately: they pack a big punch and flower prolifically. If you have tubers or very small plants, they will need to be planted during early summer, but it is possible to buy more mature plants that are in flower for immediate effect. Keep them well watered, especially in hot weather, and water them deeply: give them a really good soak.

As dahlias are such 'eye-popping' plants they really are able to stand alone, but I like to build up collections of plants, usually one type per pot, and group them together. As companions, grasses come to mind as a good foil for the dahlias; the simplicity of their foliage and habit makes them great partners for the showiness of the dahlias. I use the pheasant's tail grass (*Stipa arundinacea*) in a lot of displays. It's tough

and hardy, has a mixture of green leaves with streaks of yellow and orange, and provides movement and interest. Another favourite is *Miscanthus* 'Morning Light', a grass that I first saw at the Garden House in Devon, which is variegated and has beautiful wavy foliage that sets off nearly anything you place next to it. Even though it's described as a dwarf grass, it can grow to be quite tall (maybe a metre/39 inches), but as a potted plant adding interest to your display, it will be fine and can then be transplanted before outgrowing its welcome.

Many late-flowering perennials also make good plants for containers, and this year I have used a deep purple lobelia (*Lobelia* × *speciosa* 'Hadspen Purple') and a phlox with purple flowers (*Phlox paniculata* 'Goliath') paired with some richly coloured foliage plants to create an inviting corner on the patio. It's worth remembering that at the end of the season all these perennials can be planted out into the borders. The joy of perennials is that they keep on giving!

It's worth mentioning again that this part of the year can be very warm (unfortunately, not this year), so watering your pots is of utmost importance. Do it regularly, at least once a day in hot weather, and either early in the morning or late in the evening, making sure you really soak the pots through. And remember that

Above, left and right Beth Tarling's late summer garden is filled with chrysanthemums. Inside Beth's conservatory are potted and cut chrysanthemums and books about growing them

Above, left Dusk in late summer in Annie Stanford's glorious Somerset garden

Above, right Sunflowers, gladioli and self-seeded annuals run riot in Karen Burgess's cottage garden

as these plants are in pots, they will use up the supply of nutrients more quickly than if they had been in the border, so feed them once a week between spring and autumn (or use a long-acting fertilizer in spring that will last the whole season).

Inspiring late summer gardens

I have chosen three gardens as late summer inspiration: Longhill Carriage, Annie Stanford's garden in Somerset; Dartmoor Flower Shed, the garden of Karen Burgess in Devon; and Beth Tarling's Seaview Cottage in Cornwall.

All of them are joyfully planted cottage style gardens, and all were photographed late in summer. They have the drowsy atmosphere of the bee-laden border, perhaps a little past its prime but filled with warmth, seed heads and deep colour. And there is just a touch of the bittersweet in that there is, perhaps, an inkling that autumn is only just around the corner.

What and how to photograph in late summer

As in much of the rest of summer, I spend many hours patrolling the borders with my camera, looking for interesting viewpoints, details

and juxtapositions. Late summer presents new opportunities; just as in autumn, there are cobwebs picked out with dewdrops on most mornings, seed heads – often intricately shaped – and the play of light across the garden in the (not so early now) morning. But there are also many richly coloured flowers still blooming, and a lot of greenery which may not be there a month or so from now.

I'd like to take the opportunity to talk about photographing one particular plant in detail. Shooting border views, or small groups of plants, relies on moving around, looking for a good composition, working out what to 'crop out' in the framing and checking exactly how the light falls across the scene. Going in really close to the subject is, in truth, not much different. Ideally a macro lens is the one to use (to put it simply, macro photography is where the size of the subject in the image is life-size or even larger), but you can get close in with many modern zoom lenses or even mobile phones. You still have to look for the right composition and check what the light is doing; as a rule of thumb, keep the light to one side of you, so that it falls across the image rather than coming straight towards you or from behind. As with every 'rule' there are always exceptions, and as we discussed in an earlier chapter (see page 69), shooting directly into the light (called backlighting) can give you interesting 'bokeh' light flare; but the majority of times you will shoot with the light at 90 degrees to you. Choose a mid-range aperture, perhaps f5.6 or f8, which will give you a pleasing fall-off of focus at this distance. Anything wider (f2.8–f4) will be a little bit soft, and anything smaller (f11 or f16) will pick out more detail in the background, which can be distracting.

In photographing this sunflower, I studied the back of the plant, looking for interesting textures and patterns. As the flower goes past its prime, there are lovely striations and markings on the petals that the light has picked out, the warmth of the deep reddish-orange of the flower is vibrant, and the sepals have a graphic quality.

Left *Ammi majus* and cornflowers grow around a wooden seat in Karen Burgess's garden

Above Look out for the interesting details that make a more unusual plant portrait. Here, I have focused on the back of this sunflower and the sepals that curve backwards from the flower

SHEDS

Shed. It's a strangely emotive word and one that can bring out the romantic in many a gardener. Typically a single-storey wooden building with a roof (the term probably comes from the word 'shade'), it may originally have been a place to house animals or somewhere for the labourer to temporarily escape the heat of the day. These days, of course, a shed is more commonly used to store tools and gardening equipment, but can also be used as a workshop – or it can be a potting shed, crammed with terracotta pots, packets of seeds, dibbers and sieves. It tends to be down at heel, though it might be smart, and in a cottage garden it may well be picture-perfect. In mine, there's a radio, some bags of different potting composts, an old bathroom cabinet filled with mismatched gardening gloves, binoculars, plant labels and half-used rolls of string. And many, many spiders.

Left This corner of Beth Tarling's shed in Cornwall is being used to dry flowers and seed heads for decoration **(top left)**. Gloriously shambolic, this shed was built from recycled doors, windows and scrap timber **(top right)**. An old shepherd's hut provides a hideaway in Annie Stanford's garden **(bottom)**
Right, top The shady and cool interior of Louise and Fergus Dowding's garden shed in Somerset is used to house the collection of terracotta pots **Right, bottom** A horde of found objects, dusty paraphernalia and cobwebs in Julia Thyer's Somerset shed

AUTUMN

IN THE

COTTAGE

GARDEN

Aster 'Patricia Ballard'
and *Hylotelephium*
'Herbstfreude' in front
of *Helianthus* 'Velvet
Queen' at Bowhay
House in autumn

A snapshot of autumn at Bowhay House

There is a blissfully cool breeze in the garden today, and the unmistakable feel of autumn in the air. It has been an unusually warm summer, record-breaking in fact. And just like unseasonably wet weather, extreme heat brings with it myriad problems for the gardener. But, now, the autumn has waltzed in with cooler air and a new palette of colours. The *Verbena bonariensis* that self-seeded everywhere is still flowering, its majestic but slightly random stems waving in the wind. The oddly angular stalks are topped with purple flowers that the butterflies adore. The sunflowers ('Moulin Rouge', if I remember rightly) lasted all summer long, but are now looking a bit sorry for themselves, and I don't think I staked them well enough. This means that they tend to rock in the breeze, and the stalks do break off quite readily. Still, they can be picked up and popped in a vase for the kitchen. Many of the flowers are now seed heads, and I suspect that if I hadn't wanted the seeds, a bit of deadheading would have kept them going longer. The tomatoes have been fabulous and the beet spinach has really taken off, alongside dahlias that I bought from a plant sale at a local village fete. They have made up for lost time and are flowering their heads off!

High up above me, a buzzard is screeching and the clouds scud across an impossibly blue sky. It's a lovely day, but the lower sun and the chilly wind (and the fact that I am wearing long trousers for the first time in a while!) remind me that it's autumn and there are seeds to be collected. I take a brown paper bag and shake the dahlia seeds into it, making a note of the date, and I then carefully fold it up. The seed tin is getting full, and over winter I will take pleasure in these folded packets, planning ahead and remembering the plants that supplied them.

I spend a couple of hours bashing some recycled timber together to make a cold frame, and over the next couple of weeks I will take cuttings from the red salvias that grow so well here, with their aromatic leaves and profuse flowering. They are still in flower in mid-autumn and they are so easy to propagate. The cold frame is an important addition to any garden, and especially in spring and early summer it gives invaluable protection to tender plants and seedlings. There is nothing like making new plants for nothing, and collecting seed and taking cuttings are the bedrock of the cottage gardener's life, saving money, and giving huge satisfaction.

Right, clockwise from top left *Aster × frikartii* 'Monch'; *Rudbeckia hirta*; *Echinacea purpurea* 'Rubinstern'; *Dahlia* 'Dovegrove'

The stars of the cottage garden in autumn

After the summer, its vibrancy, long days and warmth, autumn comes along and gives us warmer colours in the garden, shorter days and a definite cooling in the air. The cottage garden is probably overflowing and a bit tired, with seed heads everywhere and a riot of hotter colours. With careful planting, though, the glory of the summer cottage garden can be extended for a month or two more. In general, the colours of spring and early summer, at the blue end of the spectrum, have been replaced with warmer yellows, oranges and reds. Late-flowering perennials are at their best now, with echinaceas, Michaelmas daisies, anemones and salvias to the fore. Dahlias, zinnias and chrysanthemums are dotted around too, and it is really a perfect time for 'cutting flowers'. And, of course, autumn is a time of plenty, with harvesting of vegetables, berries and fruit at the top of the cottage gardener's 'to do' list.

Michaelmas daisies

Michaelmas daisies, planted in groups, backlit by soft autumnal sunshine, are one of the great sights of autumn in the garden. There are many different species with a wide range of height, habit and colour. They have predominantly blue, pink and lavender shades and can form large clumps, which, on a warm autumn day attract bees and butterflies galore. Planted en masse they will give much joy through until very late in the year. In my own garden I also have *Aster amellus* 'Forncett Flourish' and *Symphyotrichum* 'Coombe Fishacre', bought from Old Court Nurseries in Malvern, mixed with *Helenium* 'Sahin's Early Flowerer', a beautiful upright orange daisy.

Dahlias

Dahlias can provide zingy colour, and are ideal for cutting and bringing into the house. They can be tricky, though, as they don't like being cold, so it's usually suggested that the tubers are uprooted in late autumn and then replanted in spring. In my garden they

are planted alongside *Leucanthemum vulgare* 'Edgeworth Giant',
which is a giant ox-eye daisy that provides interest right through
until the first frosts. Sunflowers give the almost instant height that
a new garden requires, and I leave these right up until the winter,
as the birds love the seeds. This year, a row of tomatoes provided
a seemingly endless harvest, and alongside this is one of my new
favourite plants, *Tagetes* 'Cinnabar', which is an annual African
marigold popularized by the late Christopher Lloyd at Great Dixter in
West Sussex. It is prolific, quite tall for a marigold (about 1 metre/39
inches) and has the most unusual dusky red petals with gold edging.
Tom Coward at Gravetye Manor gave me the plants and they self-
seed well, so I have a permanent supply.

William Robinson and Gertrude Jekyll, nineteenth-century
gardeners of great importance when it comes to the story of the
cottage garden, changed the way plants were used and introduced
lots of new ones that could lengthen the season of interest. The
cottage gardeners of yore would have had little or no access to
plant nurseries, so had to settle for what was readily available, but
nowadays we can prolong the season right through until the first
frost. The work of Piet Oudolf, garden designer and landscape artist,

Above This autumnal garden,
Cloud's Rest in Chepstow, is
filled with soft grasses and
colourful late perennials.
The effect is one of an
overflowing maturity

Above, left Miscanthus grass and Japanese anemones in soft backlit autumn light

Above, right Asters, rudbeckias and heleniums can be glimpsed behind the giant oat grass, *Stipa gigantea*

has popularized the use of drifts of perennial plants, especially grasses, that last through the seasons: plants that look as good in decay as they do in full flower. We can use these late-flowering perennials and grasses in our cottage gardens, and the muted colour and texture in the grasses look wonderful when placed alongside the rich reds, oranges and yellows of helenium, crocosmia and coreopsis flowers. I have placed the grasses *Miscanthus sinensis* 'Morning Light' and *Pennisetum alopecuroides* 'Hameln' in among the perennials and annuals, and the height, shape and colour of these plants provide useful punctuation marks during the quieter months of the gardening year. They also provide a link between the early summer flush of flowers in a cottage garden and the autumn showing. There can be a lull in late July or August, but the grasses and late perennials will really pull you through. I particularly love red *Salvia microphylla* – which I always take cuttings from – and *Verbena bonariensis* floating airily in front of the muted colours of a good grass.

Crab-apple and cherry trees
No garden, least of all the cottage garden, should be without a tree or two, and crab-apples fit the bill better than most. They are

generally quite small, they provide blossom, fruit and foliage (so work well in three of the four seasons) and they are much loved by our garden birds. Crab-apple jelly is a delight (try it with cheese and be forever converted!). The cottage gardeners of old would split their hard-working gardens between produce, animals and flowers, and the produce would always include fruit trees. Apples in autumn would have been a much-anticipated treat and people would have carefully stored them, wrapped in paper and stacked in boxes, away from the cold and the mice, so that they could be enjoyed through the long, dark winters.

Cherries too, can provide year-round interest, and many are available as small trees. I have a lovely cultivar (possibly *Prunus* 'Okame' – but I'm still trying to identify it for sure) that flowers its socks off in very early spring, before the leaves arrive. Its pink and pendulous blossom lights up one of our side borders. It has pretty bark, and in autumn the leaves turn a rich gold.

Mixing vegetables, herbs and flowers

I have planted rhubarb, spinach, leeks, thyme, sage and spring onions alongside the sweet pea wigwam, and this mixing of vegetables, herbs and flowers is the tell-tale sign of a real cottage garden. Runner beans can be trained up rustic plant supports, providing not only deep red flowers in summer but an edible feast into the autumn. And the sight of leeks standing in line in the autumn garden is one that few garden photographers can resist. Marrows and pumpkins are of course an autumn staple, but they do tend to take up a lot of space; some of the other squashes are fairly small and the best way to grow them is to train them over a trellis or a vertical structure. That way they not only ripen more readily, but also leave some of the ground space free. These make for lovely photographic subjects.

What to do in the autumn garden

After the busy bustle of those long summer days, autumn creeps in and suddenly it's time to stand back, assess the bigger picture and make some plans for the garden. These days a bit of untidiness is encouraged, allowing wildlife cover in the borders, and leaving some seed heads for the birds during the winter to come. However, there's plenty of exercise for those secateurs, and it helps many of the plants to have a bit of a 'haircut' before the winter winds start whistling around the beds. And don't forget, if you have a compost heap, now is the time that you will probably fill it up. It's a strangely addictive thing, filling up the compost heap. It never ceases to amaze me that however much I put in, it seems that there's still more room! People can get very enthusiastic about composting: I will never forget going to photograph a chap in Cornwall and his beautiful garden on the Lizard Peninsula. After I had spent hours shooting the place, from early morning until lunchtime, he came out of the house and asked if I had photographed 'the best bit' yet? I probably looked rather vague, so he dragged me off to a distant corner and showed me the three enormous compost bins that he had built. They were so big that he needed ladders to get up there and fill them! He seemed to take more pride in those than the rest of the (absolutely gorgeous) garden.

In late autumn, herbaceous perennials such as echinaceas, gauras and salvias will all be happy with a cut-back – but do leave a few seed heads for the birds and for some winter interest. I generally go about half-way back in autumn and then do a complete cut-back in early spring. And, as we will discuss later, seeds can be collected for next year's plants. Speaking as a garden photographer, frost-tinged seed heads of umbellifers such as cow parsley (*Anthriscus sylvestris*), and bishop's flower (*Ammi majus*) will enliven the otherwise grey-tinged days of winter. Do be careful with umbellifers, though. Some of them, angelica included, can grow into huge plants. And they are very good at seeding themselves around, so make sure to keep an eye out for their seedlings, and remove any you don't want – or don't want *there*.

Another job to wrestle with while in a tidying mood is hedge-cutting; I went for shaped hedges at the back this year and, without actually planning it, I find that the hedges now echo the hills that can be seen behind the garden. A happy accident indeed.

Autumn is also a good time to stand back and remember what was in the 'wrong' place over the summer. Move any perennials now that could do with a better position; perhaps you noticed that the lupins were crowding out the self-seeded aquilegias, or that it might be nice to place some of the gauras on the other side of a pathway so that they mirror each other? Now is the time to get on with it. Simply dig them out with plenty of soil and plant them in their new position, making sure that you water them in. As it's autumn, the plants will have a little while to bed in before the winter months. The cottage gardener is an editor, and having allowed a riot of informality in the borders, is careful to edit the plants so that this appearance is kept up but carefully managed.

Right, clockwise from top left Lifting dahlias for storage over winter; planting a layered pot of tulip bulbs; pruning a rose; planting crocus bulbs in autumn

I have just spent a joyous morning digging up self-seeded aquilegias, lupins and larkspurs, potting them in small terracotta pots, ready to reposition them in spring.

    One of the best things about autumn is buying and planting bulbs that will flower in spring. The still-warm soil means that the bulbs bed in well, and later on your hard work is repaid in full, as a sudden burst of colour heralds the coming of spring. Daffodils, crocuses, tulips, fritillaries and grape hyacinths can all be planted, as can some hardy later flowers such as alliums and lilies. A drift of alliums meandering through an early summer border is a sight to behold, so it's worth buying and planting as many as you can afford. As with most bulbs, the rule is to plant them at least three or four times the depth of the size of the bulb, so for alliums about 15 cm/6 inches is ideal. Most hardy bulbs, including tulips and daffodils, come from areas with dry summer climates, so prefer a warm, sunny site with good drainage. Also, it tends to look more impressive if the bulbs are planted in fairly dense groups: thirty or forty together look much better than a sparse sprinkling.

    There is plenty to do in the vegetable patch too: garlic can be planted now, along with lettuce, chard, beetroot and radish. The

Above Planting allium bulbs in autumn for flowering the following summer

Above Broad bean seeds are best planted in root trainer pots, as the beans need a long root run

early cottage gardeners would pack their patches with produce (with flowers alongside), but during the nineteenth century, as gardening became more of a pastime than a way of living, flowers tended to become more important. Still, we all know how much nicer home-grown vegetables taste than those you find in the supermarket, and planting colourful ruby chard, for instance, works on two levels – it looks as good as it tastes. Sow the seeds in early autumn and you can be harvesting the young leaves by the beginning of winter. The same goes for beetroot and radish. Perhaps my favourite of all vegetables is the broad bean, and autumn is a good time to get these going, too. They are seemingly indestructible even in a bad winter, and come the spring autumn-sown broad beans seem to be more resistant to blackfly.

Autumn is the perfect time to improve your soil. Having cleared away some of the growth of summer, it's easier to see what you are doing, so you can now mulch and feed the soil. I prefer to dig as little as possible, so I mulch the borders with fresh compost, either from my own bin or from bought products. The addition of a mulch layer not only adds nutrients back into the soil, but acts as a blanket during the winter weather. Your plants will thank you with extra and more vital growth come the spring.

Lastly for the autumn jobs, and definitely among the most important, is the collection of seeds. Apart from getting free plants next year, the satisfaction gained from collecting and growing on those new plants is enormous; it really is life-affirming to feel that connection with the earth and the joy from taking a minute seed and ushering it into the following year as a new plant. All to be repeated again the next year. The simplest way to collect is to keep an eye on the plant and when the seed head is dried out and ready to disperse its bounty, pop it in a brown paper bag and give it a shake. The seeds should fall out into the bag. Then label it with the plant name and date collected. One of the great joys to be had on a cold midwinter day is shuffling through those many paper bags, organizing your seed box and thinking about when and where to sow them.

Below, left A lovely haul: seeds collected from *Tagetes* 'Cinnabar' in autumn

Below, right Seed heads can be as beautiful as the flowers from which they came. These poppy seed heads are an architectural wonder

A ROUND-UP OF
AUTUMN JOBS

1   Buy and plant bulbs for next spring and summer. Most spring-flowering bulbs can be planted by the end of September, but tulips should go in later, perhaps in November.

2   Sow hardy annuals for next year. An autumn sowing can survive frost, and the plants will be bigger next year than those sown in the early spring.

3   Clip hedges. It's best to wait until the summer growth has slowed down, so October or November is ideal.

4   Improve the soil: in particular, mulch the ground. This will keep weeds down and add nutrition to the soil.

5   Sow vegetables, especially chard, radish and broad beans.

6   Rehouse tender plants before the first frosts, Take softwood cuttings of tender perennials. Plants such as pelargoniums, pinks, penstemons and salvia should root reliably in the autumn.

7   Divide and cut back perennials. Move and edit as necessary.

8   Plant trees and shrubs in autumn: this gives them a while to settle in and get a good start in the following spring.

9   Harvest any vegetables that are ready, e.g., tomatoes, runner beans, potatoes, carrots and many salad leaves.

10   Collect seeds; label and store carefully.

A PROJECT FOR AN AUTUMN DAY

Planting a crab-apple tree

(clockwise from top left)

Dig a hole big enough and deep enough for the rootball to fit comfortably

Check the rootball is at the correct depth (level with the ground)

Step carefully around the tree, making sure that the soil is firmly in contact with the roots

Backfill with the soil up to the top of the rootball

Left This collection of daisies, dahlias, cosmos and lantanas works perfectly in old terracotta pots at Great Dixter

Below, left Mint can be planted in pots around the garden (and the pot helps prevent it becoming invasive)

Below, right This selection of autumn containers at Bowhay House captures the warmth and texture of the season

Cottage containers in autumn

After the excitement and explosion of colour that is summer, it's nice to keep the interest going into the cooler months. A grouping of autumn containers near to the back door, or perhaps in a corner of the patio, can be a real boost as the days draw in.

When choosing which container to use, remember that you will need a good strong one to withstand the autumnal chill, perhaps terracotta or wood. And think about the design of the pot when choosing the plants. One big 'hero' plant at the back can be fronted up with some foliage or flowers, and a trailing ivy at the front can finish the look. Don't forget that pots at this time of year benefit from being raised off the ground with 'pot feet', which ensure that water doesn't gather and cause the roots to get cold and waterlogged. And the compost you use is important too. A good peat-free John Innes is the best choice as it's fairly heavy (being loam-based) and holds nutrients and moisture better than a lighter compost.

Foliage plants are a perfect foil for flowers, There are ferns, of course, and all sorts of silver foliage plants such as santolina, helichrysum and cineraria. If you choose a metal container

(I have a selection of old tin buckets, for example), you will find that the silvery foliage plants echo the metal rather well. Variegated euonymus always works as a backdrop to more colourful flowers, and heucheras provide a wide range of foliage colours that keep going for ages.

Herbs are a great choice for an autumn container. Thyme, mint or sage, for instance, will stay on through the winter and if near enough to the kitchen can be picked regularly for cooking. There are even some colourful small salads that can be planted: oak-leaved lettuce, for example, is excellent grown in a container, and you can 'cut and come again' for many weeks.

In terms of flowers, there are some exquisite small violas, and these, mixed with a foliage plant or two, can last for a long time. I try to keep away from the violently coloured pansies in the garden centres, as I find that a carefully selected collection of muted colours at the same end of the palette looks much smarter.

There are some great perennial plants that work in an autumn container, not least the asters (now named *Symphyotrichum*), of which the 'New York' or 'novi-belgii' types, which are smaller in habit, are best. They come in a range of pinks and blues and keep on flowering for a long time. And the chocolate cosmos is another long flowerer: it looks lovely backed by a grass, its near-black flowers contrasting particularly well with the thin and spiky foliage of a miscanthus. One of the great things about using perennials in containers is that once you decide to swap over your container display, or do a seasonal revamp, the plants can be popped into the border to carry on giving value for many more months, or even years.

Finally, there are bulbs that flower in autumn – but do remember that these obviously need to be planted in spring or summer unless you buy plants that are already flowering. Colchicums, cyclamens and nerines are all fabulous in pots, and can either be left in the pot or replanted in the appropriate area of the garden afterwards.

An inspiring autumn garden

Gravetye Manor, Sussex

For many reasons, it's a magical experience visiting the garden at Gravetye. This is the home of William Robinson, 'father' of the modern cottage garden, and a hands-on and practical gardener who was hugely influential through his books and magazine articles.

Above all, though, Gravetye is a beautifully planted garden which delights at every season. In autumn, it shines. Tom Coward,

Right Billowing autumn borders at Gravetye Manor

Tom Coward, the current head gardener, is an admirer of Robinson, but has introduced new plants and rejuvenated the borders and the kitchen garden since he moved there from Great Dixter.

In autumn the borders are billowing and graceful with not a patch of bare earth to be seen. Dahlias, marigolds, tithonia and roses compete for the sun, and on a misty morning the grasses that are stitched between the flowers are adorned with cobwebs and dewdrops. There are also surprises: a bank of ginger lilies lines a path that has views of the rather imposing manor house, and a pretty summerhouse with a tiled roof can be seen at the end of a cottage style paved path. The view is almost obscured by the banks of orange dahlias, copper marigolds and mauve phlox.

In a small side garden, much more cosy and intimate, an oak-framed outbuilding is surrounded by autumn planting, the stars of which are the asters and Russian sage that are placed among huge stands of grasses. Angel's fishing rods (*Dierama pulcherrima*) are going to seed too, and the sense is of a garden at full maturity, perhaps a little past its summer glory but still putting on a show.

Left The paved path that leads through the small side garden at Gravetye Manor is planted with grasses and autumn colour

Above Virginia creeper climbing over the porch

Over the back door of the house is a porch that carries a fabulous Virginia creeper (*Parthenocissus quinquefolia*) burning with a red hue that is hard to imagine in any other context. Pure autumn.

The borders at Gravetye are full of surprises throughout the year. The usual favourite cottage garden classics are there in abundance; lady's mantle (*Alchemilla mollis*) edges the paved path, but joy of joys, a self-seeded plantain (*Plantago media*) is allowed to stay alongside. Plantain is often considered a 'weed', but, as we know, William Robinson himself was keen to use wild plants in the garden (one of his biggest-selling books was *The Wild Garden*). And plantain is a rather beautiful plant when you look at it; here, self-seeded and not edited out, it typifies the cottage garden approach. There on its own merit, it softens the paving and has an architectural quality which is unnoticed when you see the plant in the middle of a lawn or field.

What and how to photograph in autumn

Autumn, as Keats said, is the season of 'mists and mellow fruitfulness' and, as a garden photographer, I look forward to those softly lit days when reds, oranges and yellows all shine out. The days are getting shorter (I no longer have to get up at an ungodly hour to get to a garden by 5.30 a.m.) and the light is kinder, so we lose those harsh highlights and deep blacks in an image. There are swallows twittering around the house and there is plenty to look out for in the garden: seed heads and fallen leaves, cobwebs and rosehips, and moody views across bountiful borders.

Look for a simple composition, and keep an eye out for a strong focal point. So, imagine a backlit garden fork left in the recently dug vegetable patch, a few fresh potatoes beneath. Or a long view down a cobbled path, a watering can left alongside some late-flowering perennials, or an architectural feature such as a birdbath festooned with dewdrop-hung cobwebs. Go close in and look for detail. The translucent seed heads of honesty, one of the classic cottage self-seeders, for example. Or the rich tones of a dahlia in full flow. The cactus varieties have amazing petals that one can spend hours studying.

If you have a proper camera, use a wide aperture, perhaps f4, and you will get a narrow depth of field. This helps put the background out of focus and makes the subject stand out. If you are using a mobile phone you can download certain apps that enable this too. The wider aperture also means that you can use a faster shutter speed, which helps in lower light situations. As I'm always saying, I try to use a tripod at all times in order to reduce camera shake, but with certain cameras these days, there is a system within the camera body or lens whereby shake is much reduced. Try to get the feel of the garden. It's autumn and it's got a certain atmosphere, so aim for a softly lit and romantic look to your pictures. It really is the most magical time.

Above *Dahlia merckii* captured though a wide aperture, to ensure it stands out against the background

Right A spider's web with its weaver in the autumn light

COMPOST

The very word 'compost' is enough to get a gardener's pulse racing. I have met gardeners who are more excited showing me their compost heaps than their beautifully tended borders (for an example, see page 146). It can seem an inexact and somewhat mysterious science, but compost is the lifeblood of a fertile garden, and the end product from a good compost heap is truly 'black gold'.

At its simplest, composting waste material from the garden, or from the kitchen, is a simple procedure. When organic materials decompose properly, you end up with compost, which looks like garden soil and is full of nutrients. The process involves mixing organic material with carbon and those with nitrogen, as well as a lot of air and water, usually in a heap or in a bin. The job of composting is done by organisms such as worms and insects, but also, more importantly, by micro-organisms which cause the decay of the material by eating and then excreting it. The gardener can speed the process up by shredding the material before it goes into the heap and by adding water and air. Making compost is good for the garden soil and saves you money. It also saves using commercially made fertilizers which can contain lots of chemicals. Moreover, it is environmentally friendly, as it prevents materials from ending up in landfills, where they take up space and emit powerful greenhouse gases such as methane.

The recipe for good compost is fairly simple: it is all about the balance of four ingredients, water, air, nitrogen (sometimes called 'greens') and carbon (sometimes called 'browns'). Heaps

that include an excessive amount of nitrogen-rich material ('greens') are likely to be too wet and smell bad; if your heap contains too much carbon-rich material ('browns') it will get dry and take a long time to decompose. Either is easy to fix by introducing carbon- or nitrogen-rich material, depending on what you need for a balance.

Examples of 'greens' are fresh organic waste, lawn mowings and food waste, and examples of 'browns' are dead leaves, twigs and paper. A rule of thumb for achieving the perfect carbon-to-nitrogen ratio in your home compost is to include two to four parts of brown materials for each part of green materials. Air and water can easily be added: turn the pile once a week in summer,

Above A well-kept compost area is a thing of beauty – and the sign of a good gardener

and maybe once a month in winter, and give the whole thing a good watering once in a while.

There is nothing more satisfying than using your own compost on the garden: it feels, then, that the circle is complete.

Through the seasons

WINTER

IN THE

COTTAGE

GARDEN

A hazel wigwam adds structure to frosted winter borders

A snapshot of winter at Bowhay House

The flag over the nearby pub, The Pig's Nose Inn, is no longer horizontal in the wind, and there is a break in the iron-grey sky; icy bullets of wintry rain have abated, and the brief respite has allowed me out to take a look at the rather drab-looking and sodden borders. Winter can be breathtakingly beautiful, with frosty outlines picked out in a low sun, or it can be, as now, a limited palette of ochre, dull green and a multitude of greys. We have had it all this year, weather-wise, but on close inspection the garden has stood up remarkably well: there are some spikes of green poking up between the stumps of cut-back perennials, bulbs are appearing here and there and there's even some new growth in the clumps of sweet william that I grew from seed last spring. *Helleborus niger*, the Christmas rose, is resplendent in my tin tub containers, surrounded by the dark foliage of heucheras that set it off well. *Euphorbia characias* is in its pomp, looking dramatic against the black-painted shiplap shed, its nodding, dusky green heads seemingly immune to frost and rain. Among the camassias that are re-emerging beneath a just-budding cherry tree are more hellebores, the oriental hybrids this time, their new flower heads just visible. I'm reminded that the old leaves need cutting back – a favourite winter job, as there's great satisfaction in cutting back the old to reveal new growth and the flower buds that herald a new season. The green shoots of snowdrops are just showing – I am always amazed at how these delicate flowers can first push through the frosty ground and then withstand the perils of winter.

A lone red campion (*Silene dioica*) flower from a self-seeded plant is a beacon of light at the back of the shady border – a wintry reminder of where we are. Red campion is a prolific plant that needs to be kept in check – the lanes and hedgerows of South Devon are festooned with it during early summer – but this lone outlier is a welcome addition to the border. Self-seeding, whether of wild or 'garden' plants, is key to the apparently 'random' nature of the cottage garden (but the good gardener will learn to edit and control these plants so that the garden doesn't get overwhelmed by the stronger ones).

The stars of the cottage garden in winter

Think of a cottage garden and you'd be forgiven for picturing summer in all its fulsomeness, billowing borders jammed with colour, scent and, above all, flowers. However, the cottage garden can also shine in deepest midwinter. On a dreary day nothing gladdens the heart more than the first sight of irises, crocus and snowdrops bravely, and somewhat incongruously, flowering above the otherwise lifeless-looking soil.

One of the first jobs I did on digging out my new borders was to sprinkle handfuls of tiny crocus and iris bulbs beneath the earth. Three months later (and now again, another year on), the spikes of green reach for the sky and are a joyful reminder that the seasons, and the garden, move onwards. My favourites are the little green sword-like leaves of crocus, with their distinctive white midrib, followed by glorious cup-shaped flowers that often have a bewitching scent. *Crocus* 'Snow Bunting', bought in bagsful, is just perfect, especially mixed with taller, and perhaps more elegant, *Iris* 'Harmony' and I. 'Purple Whitewell'.

Of course, one mustn't forget snowdrops. I was given fifty bulbs of the common snowdrop (*Galanthus nivalis*), and these have set up home in a shady border near the conservatory. Over time, they will fill out and spread, creating a drift of pearly white and deliciously scented flowers.

East Lambrook Manor in Somerset, a spiritual home of the cottage garden, is a mecca for snowdrop lovers (otherwise known as galanthophiles), and a visit in February is a must if you're able to get there. There are swathes of this little bulb as far as the eye can see, swirling beneath witch hazels with their spidery yellow flowers. The other cottage garden favourite in winter is of course the hellebore, the earliest of which is the Christmas rose, *Helleborus niger*, with its delicate, nodding white flower heads that look good in clumps. Later, the oriental hellebore, *Helleborus × hybridus*, emerges in its bewildering variety of patterns and colours, bred over many years by specialist nurseries.

Shrubs are, of course, the backbone of many a garden, but the cottage garden, usually a small plot, may have room for only a few.

Left, clockwise from top left
Galanthus 'Atkinsii'; *Skimmia japonica* 'Godrie's Dwarf'; *Iris* 'Katharine Hodgkin'; *Daphne* 'Spring Beauty'

Above A terracotta urn swaddled in lichen can be a focal point, as can a frosted seed head

Flowering shrubs such as witch hazel or, in my case, skimmia, can provide some winter interest and wildlife support too. Berries are a welcome food source for visiting birds, especially the thrushes; hollies are invaluable and even the humble ivy can supply late nectar for butterflies and bees, as well as dark clusters of berries which the birds love. A winter-flowering honeysuckle, *Lonicera fragrantissima*, attracts insects that the birds then feed on, and, as an added bonus, it smells sublime. Daphnes, too, are particularly fragrant shrubs – especially 'Jacqueline Postill', which will stop you in your tracks with its heady scent.

As the cottage garden can be a veritable larder for wildlife, it's worth planning for a few shrubs and even small trees that not only look good but are helpful for our wild friends. We were lucky enough to inherit an old and magnificent hawthorn tree when we moved here. It's always full of birds, and I have encouraged a noisy bunch of blue tits by putting up a bird box within the tree. My sister gave me a crab-apple, *Malus* 'John Downie', on a 'significant' birthday, and this is the perfect small cottage garden tree. Although it's not much to look at in winter, it has beautiful flowers in spring, and amazing and profuse fruit in autumn. Great for the wildlife, lovely to look at and with the promise of crab-apple jelly in years to come.

Cottage garden focal points in winter

When planning and designing any garden, it is important to think about the structures upon which the planting hangs. The flower beds at Gravetye, for example, are anchored by the sundial at the garden's centre, while at Barnsley House in the Cotswolds, the alliums and tulips beside the paved path are perfectly set off by the magnificent golden tendrils of the laburnum tunnel above. The cottage garden, being a more homespun affair, relies on quieter and more rustic structures, but they can still have a similar effect. In winter, these structures are particularly important: a cleverly placed terracotta pot, urn or rhubarb forcer will pull an otherwise empty and rather lifeless border together; seed heads on tall plants make excellent focal points, as do hazel wigwams stripped of summer climbers, a bench placed at the end of a paved path, or even just a rickety wooden potting shed door hung with horseshoes found in the soil. All or any of these can become significant points in the canvas on which frost can paint a picture. A winter morning with the sun piercing the mist and highlighting the frost-frilled leaves or – all too rare here – virgin snow is enough to get even the laziest of us out into the garden to marvel at its beauty.

The design of the garden at Bowhay is simple, with its diagonal crossed paths between the borders, but the addition of rose arches gives a sightline which takes the eye to the corner, where a simple tin trough provides a focal point. The rest of the garden is structured around the sightline so that, even in winter, there is height, and simple features to catch the eye: a rhubarb forcing pot, an old chimney and a tall hazel wigwam, for example. As winter ends and the first spring bulbs arrive, the stage is set for a new performance.

What to do in the winter garden

Winter can be a quiet time in any garden, but there is still plenty to do if, like me, you have overdone it at Christmas and feel the need for fresh air and some good honest toil to assuage the guilt! Even tidying the shed can be cathartic, while trawling the seed catalogues, ticking off the 'most wanted', is mood-enhancing. I enjoy sorting my containers, brushing them out and organizing them by size. This is also a good time to clean down the shelves and wash the windows. You should check for any necessary repairs such as sharpening and oiling tools, tying up the used bamboo canes, and recycling any broken pots to use as crocks in newly planted containers.

Outside, there are plenty of jobs to be done: mending any static plant supports (I have a permanent hazel wigwam that needed a bit of TLC this year), cutting back perennials and pruning shrubs. Plant up a winter container or two – the combinations of foliage and colour that even this season offers can keep some interest until spring.

It's a good idea to sweep up leaves from paths and terraces as it stops them being slippery, but try to leave a few around the backs of borders, as the insects love to hide beneath them. If you have room, the leaves can be kept in a holey bin bag for a year to provide a lovely leafmould soil conditioner.

Protect any container plants if freezing weather is forecast, and check whether any need watering (watch out for evergreens, especially). If they have been moved into a more sheltered area, they may be out of the rain, so it's worth being vigilant.

I find that winter is a good time to take a real look at the borders and check what may need to be moved, or what gaps need to be filled – they are at their most stripped-back at this time of year, so it's easier to see the general layout now. Much of the deadheading

Right The jobs of tidying, maintaining and generally sorting in the shed provide welcome breaks during cold, dark winter days

and moving of plants will have been completed in the autumn, but any seed heads that have been left for the birds and wildlife can be checked, and tidied up if need be.

There are a few winter seed sowings that can be done; I have just sown marigolds, poppies, hollyhocks and larkspur, and, as a cottage garden simply must have sweet peas, now is the time for some early sowings. Put them in deep pots (or, better still, root-trainers), as legumes (such as peas and beans) have deep roots, and then place them under cover; a little heat helps, so a propagator may be useful, but it is not essential, and even without heat they should be showing in about ten days.

Roses and other shrubs can be pruned at this time of year. Use your newly sharpened secateurs, and prune out any crossing or rubbing stems as well as dead or weak branches. When pruning roses, try to cut just above an outward-facing bud, so that the plant grows outwards and has a more 'open-centre' look. As always, it's useful and wise to look up pruning techniques for specific plants, as what works with one may not be right for another.

Above Make sure you plant tulip bulbs by Christmas, if possible

A ROUND-UP OF WINTER JOBS

1 Feed birds: provide fatballs or hanging nut feeders and suitable seeds; they will even appreciate uncooked bacon rind.

2 Tidy up perennials: cut back straggly plant stems and spent flowers, but be sure to leave some seed heads for the birds.

3 Turn compost over, making sure that you 'layer' your heap (you can even use cardboard, as long as it's torn up).

4 'Comb' grasses to remove dead leaves: the grasses will look better and the dead foliage can go on the compost heap.

5 Prune roses, cutting back by no more than a third. Take out crossing branches and any dead wood.

6 Cut back hellebores, to allow the new growth to show up well in the next few months.

7 Sharpen tools and tidy the shed, clean down surfaces and wash any windows. Organize your old pots – and sweep the floor!

8 Ensure that your tulip bulbs are planted by Christmas, if possible. They can go in later, but early winter is the ideal time.

9 Sow sweet peas in winter, to be ready for a super show the following year.

10 If you like, make a winter wreath, using evergreen foliage and any berries you have in the garden.

A PROJECT FOR A WINTER DAY

Sowing sweet peas

(clockwise from top left)

Adding a little sand to general-purpose peat-free compost to make a nice, light mix

Sowing the sweet pea seeds

Young sweet peas being grown on

Encouraging germination in a propagator

Left Snowdrops and *Iris*
'Harmony' planted together
in old terracotta pots and a
reused tomato tin

Above Planting up orange
polyanthus plants in an old
tin bucket and pairing with
Euphorbia characias

Cottage containers in winter

Pots filled with colourful or scented winter interest plants provide
mood-lifting cheer during the darker months. They are easy to
create and require minimum maintenance. Place them outside
the back door, so that you can enjoy them without having to get
cold and wet. Evergreen foliage plants, herbs, bulbs and bedding
combine to make a show as lovely as any that you get in spring or
summer. Obviously, in past times, the cottage gardener would have
been focused on the practical side of things, but I like to think that
even then, the cottagers would have filled a few pots with whatever
flowers they could muster, perhaps digging up some snowdrops
and a stray spurge.

There are definite considerations for these colder months: first,
choose the right container – go for 'frost-resistant' pots if using
terracotta, stone or composite materials, as otherwise they can
crack as they freeze and unfreeze. Perhaps think about wooden
'half-barrels', which offer greater protection to delicate plant
roots as temperatures drop. You can even use recycled household
containers; old tin cans (large Italian tomato tins from friendly
neighbourhood restaurants, for example) can look great filled

with early spring bulbs. The old cottage gardeners reused broken teacups, teapots, holey watering cans and disused wheelbarrows as plant containers.

Next, ensure that you have the right growing medium. Always use fresh compost, as old compost is generally lacking in nutrients and may harbour pests or disease. Make sure you have the right type too – a general-purpose compost is fine for most plants, but do check what soil your plants need. For example, acid-loving plants such as camellias and gaultherias require ericaceous compost. Whatever type of compost you use, it will probably be worth mixing in a little grit to improve drainage. Always make sure there are drainage holes at the bottom of your pots. And I would recommend raising the pots on either 'pot feet' or just some evenly sized stones. Plants hate sitting in cold, waterlogged containers.

When planting up your pots, be sure to position your new plants at the right depth (usually the same as that of the pots they originally came in) – and don't worry too much about giving them room to grow: during winter they don't grow much anyway, so you can pack them in. Firm down the compost and cover the whole pot with some mulch – perhaps grit, bark or pebbles – to prevent rain splashes. This will also help to cut water loss by evaporation and stop weeds from germinating. Don't forget to place your pots in a sunny position – and it's nice to have them near the door.

As, at this time of year, most plants won't grow as much as during spring or summer, you will need to choose some that are already a good size. A bit of height for the back of the display, perhaps a conifer or a small shrub, and maybe something like an ivy to spill down the front. I like to pop in a few spring bulbs beneath everything, so that the whole show keeps going. A conifer has year-round interest, but I prefer small shrubs with nice foliage, perhaps box, bay, skimmia or pittosporum – or sarcococca (Christmas box), which is both an evergreen and also has sweet-smelling flowers. Grasses provide texture and colour, while many ferns have attractive evergreen foliage. Some perennial plants are useful too: heucheras have evergreen or semi-evergreen foliage in green or rich plum shades, some with exquisite markings; and many heathers provide good colour through the winter months.

An inspiring winter garden

East Lambrook Manor Garden is internationally renowned as a mecca of cottage gardening. The gardener and writer Margery Fish made her home there and developed the garden during the 1940s, 1950s and 1960s. Mrs Fish was a late starter to gardening but even as a novice she had a brilliant eye for colour and form, and she epitomized the approach of the cottage gardener, using simple everyday flowers abundantly planted and with a refreshing lack of formality. As she says in one of her books, *Cottage Garden Flowers*, published in 1961, 'Nowhere in the world is there anything like the English cottage garden. In every village and hamlet in the land there are these little gardens, always gay and never garish, and so obviously loved. There are not so many now, alas, as those cottages of cob or brick, with their thatched roofs and tiny crooked windows, are disappearing to make way for council houses and modern bungalows, but the flowers remain, flowers that have come to be known as "cottage flowers" because of their simple, steadfast qualities.'

East Lambrook has passed through the hands of various owners, but the garden has always remained fundamentally a cottage garden.

Below On a winter's day at East Lambrook Manor, snowdrops around an old wooden water butt and a drift of *Crocus tommasinianus* beneath the variegated sycamore *Acer pseudoplatanus* 'Leopoldii' catch the morning sun

Above Get down low when photographing small plants such as these hellebores. It pays to look up at the flowers

These days it is popular throughout the seasons, and winter, which is a tricky season for most gardens, is actually one of the best times to visit East Lambrook. It puts on a fantastic snowdrop show, and the typical cottage features that dot the garden are the perfect foil for the wintry scene. An old wine barrel used as a water butt is a picture-perfect sight with clumps of snowdrops beneath. There is an excellent small nursery, and a wonderful tea-shop too!

What and how to photograph in winter

Photography in the winter garden can be tricky, particularly if you are shooting bulbs, as they are usually so low to the ground. My advice would be to get down on all fours so that the camera or the phone is right down at ground level (I recommend buying knee pads and wearing clothes that you don't mind getting dirty). It's good to see the shape of the whole plant, so you need to be low down. And, when looking at hellebores and snowdrops, as the flower heads generally point downwards, you should be pointing your lens up.

Choose a still day (not so easy in midwinter), as the slightest breath of wind can make for a blurry image. As I'm always saying, I recommend using a tripod in the garden, so that the camera doesn't shake, but If you have a steady hand, you can hand-hold. This is useful in getting down low and looking up into the flower, and I find it also helps to use a white sheet of card or paper to bounce some light back up into the flower head.

These days, though, if you are a bit more serious about your photography, it's quite easy to use your camera software to lighten areas of the image. In terms of settings, if you have a decent camera that can change aperture and shutter speeds, try a wide aperture for shallow depth of field – it can really make for an interesting image, with lovely soft petals surrounding pin-sharp stamens in the middle.

LET NATURE IN

As I scrabble around at the back of a border, I spot the small pink flower of herb robert (*Geranium robertianum*) and its finely cut foliage sprawling across sun-dappled earth. Known sometimes as 'Stinky Bob', this is an unobtrusive plant, but an important source of food and nectar for many bees and hoverflies.

And, a little further on, among a stand of foxgloves, is the unmistakably huge emerging leaf of a hogweed. Now, in former times, certainly at my last garden (in a town), I would have grabbed both of these plants and wrenched them out; not now, though. I have come to appreciate what some will call 'weeds'. I still edit carefully, but I am taking care to leave some of them. I love these rather beautiful native plants, and have realized that they have a place in the scheme of things.

Have you ever seen a common hogweed (*Heracleum sphondylium*), 1.8 metres/6 feet tall in midsummer, covered with hoverflies? It is a sight to behold, and indeed to treasure. (Don't confuse it, though, with giant hogweed, *Heracleum mantegazzianum*, which is an invasive bad boy and can be harmful.) Growing out of the top of our wall is another umbellifer, alexanders (*Smyrnium olusatrum*); this is edible (the seeds

Left Here, cow parsley (*Anthriscus sylvestris*) seems to be breaking in through the garden gate

Right, top Alexanders (*Smyrnium olusatrum*) on top of our garden wall

Right, bottom Shining geranium (*Geranium lucidum*) in the borders with *Centaurea nigra*

taste like black pepper, the roots like parsnip and the stem, a bit like broccoli): a spring bloomer that loves a sea breeze, it does well around here.

In a shady border beneath the cherry tree is garlic mustard (or Jack-by-the-hedge – *Alliaria petiolata*) which has been held back by some careful but not total editing, and red campion (*Silene dioica*), both of which are happy in this cooler and more shaded situation, and hold their own alongside other more traditional garden plants. The campion is great for filling gaps while waiting for the later camassias and Japanese anemones (*Anemone × hybrida*) to flower. As I write this at the end of summer, it's still flowering away in the shade of the cherry tree. And at the very front of the border is shining geranium (*Geranium lucidum*), with its small pink flowers and shiny foliage. If it stays until late summer, its foliage, and the stems, go deep red; in my eyes, it outshines all the 'proper' flowers behind it.

The common denominator with many of these native plants is their value as pollinators (where would we be without pollinators for our tomatoes, apples, and next year's supply of seeds for the garden?) and as a food source for the caterpillars that become the next generation of butterflies and moths. These insects in turn support the birds and are part of a healthy ecosystem. And it's not just birds that eat insects. They're an important part of the diet of hedgehogs, spiders, bats, fish, frogs and toads. There are even some insects, including wasps,

Left, top Early bumblebees love the spring crocuses

Left, bottom Common hogweed covered with hoverflies in summer

ladybirds, and ants, that eat other insects.

For so long we have tried to eradicate 'weeds' by blasting them with chemicals, or we have paved and tarmacked the land. We have even tried to get rid of grass lawns and replace them with plastic grass! We have tried to get rid of garden 'pests' with killing sprays and we tidy up the autumn borders so much that the insects and invertebrates have nowhere to go. The balance of nature has been lost in our gardens, and as they make up a significant part of our land-mass (in the UK the garden area is more than four and a half times that of that of our National Nature Reserves), we really are doing some damage. Fortunately, it seems that we may have turned the corner (or reached the bottom!), and the popularity of the RSPB's 'Garden Birdwatch' or Plantlife's 'No Mow May' (see page 188) indicates that modern gardeners are more aware of the issues than in previous years.

How can we help? The cottage garden could easily be, and traditionally would have been, a nature-friendly garden. We love the self-seeders, the jumble of plants, the wild or native plants that help create diversity. If a cottage garden is planted with constant interest for the gardener (or for the garden photographer!), even in late autumn and winter there would be flowers available for pollen. (I'm often surprised at the number of early bees that visit snowdrops and crocuses in late winter.) So, if we can plant with that in mind, we will help nurture the wildlife. As it also nurtures us. We *all* want to see flowers and interest all year round, so a parade of snowdrops, followed by tulips, forget-me-nots, alliums, then roses, dahlias, sunflowers and

Right, top Even tiny ponds are great for wildlife

Right, bottom Hedgehogs crossing!

asters, and yet more snowdrops, keeps us all going through the year.

A good structure of cottage shrubs gives us a framework; These structural plants can hold their own in the winter months, when herbaceous perennials lie dormant below ground. Look for those that have good blossom and fruits during the quieter seasons and the wildlife will be grateful. And keep the seasonal interest going by planting seeds successively, so that the flowers come in waves, rather than all at once. The typical cottage garden 'jumble' of flowers, all mixed together, is beneficial too and means that a wide range of insects is attracted. In terms of plant types, it's a good thing to have as many siingle-flowered plants as possible (double flowers are not so good for insect life, as they find it harder to get to the pollen).

We can build a pond. One of the best ways to support wildlife, a pond can be whatever size suits your garden, from a simple bucket or old sink sunk into the ground, to a much larger, properly lined and planted pond. Water is one of the best ways to encourage wildlife; from birds that come to bathe, to frogs, newts, dragonflies and even grass snakes that come for the shelter, the water and the food, And, by the way, the addition of a pond is also good for us: it's fascinating, it's calming and it's rather beautiful. With plenty of photographic possibilities too!

A log pile is an excellent way to attract insects and a convenient way to get rid of unwanted wood cuttings. The insects use the pile as home and larder, and, along with fungi, they help to break down the wood over time. Place the pile in some shade (I have one at the back of a

deep border and it's virtually invisible now). It's attractive to insects and therefore hedgehogs – and I saw a hedgehog in this garden for the first time earlier this year. (You would not believe how excited I was!) It goes without saying that if you want to keep your hedgehogs, allow them in and out of the garden by providing access holes in hedges or fences – and do not use slug pellets, which are poisonous to all wildlife.

Resist the temptation to mow the lawn once a week, and let the grass grow. Plantlife (a brilliant charity that looks after our native plants in the UK) has a campaign to allow the lawns and green spaces to grow for a month in May. This helps the pollinators, it tackles pollution and it helps lock atmospheric carbon below ground. You will be amazed at how many wild flowers emerge in your lawn areas: beautiful flowers, sedges and native grasses will pop up, even if you let it go for just a few short weeks in summer. And if you can wait until late summer to cut it back ('Let it bloom in June!'), the flowers will have had a chance to seed themselves and you'll get even more next year. We in the UK have lost 97 per cent of our flower-rich meadows since the 1970s and with them the vital food needed by pollinators. This is a way that we can help restore some of the balance.

Give the birds some boxes and they will nest. My own box is halfway up the hawthorn tree and has, since the first week I put it up, been a home for the blue tits in my garden. They seem to thrive there, and are very good at getting rid of the aphids that seem to love my lupins.

Finally, be organic. Don't use chemicals to kill so-called pests or weeds. Let nature do its job: it's much better at it than we are.

Right Mr Brazil down the road in our village has a garden that he describes as 'built for wildlife'. It's packed with wild flowers, and apart from an occasional trim, allowed to bloom unhindered

RESOURCES

Agriframes
Classic hand-crafted
garden structures
www.agriframes.co.uk
+44 (0)117 934 1790

David Austin
English Roses
www.davidaustinroses.co.uk
+44 (0)1902 376300

Avon Bulbs
Leading bulb specialist
www.avonbulbs.co.uk
+44 (0)1460 242 177

Cambo Gardens
Snowdrop suppliers
www.cambogardens.org.uk
+44 (0)1333 451 040

Haws
Watering cans
www.haws.co.uk
+44 (0)121 420 2494

Niwaki
Japanese gardening equipment
www.niwaki.com
+44 (0) 1747445059

Old Court Nurseries
Specialists in Michaelmas
daisies since 1906
www.autumnasters.co.uk
+44 (0)1684 540416

Stone Willow
Hand-crafted willow by
Sue Radford
+44 (0)1803 712498

ACKNOWLEDGEMENTS

This project would not have been possible without the support and help of my wife, Sarah. She understood when it may have seemed that the progress of the garden was more important to me than the house renovations! Lots of love to her and many, many thanks. (Unfortunately, now that this is finished, I need to don my painting clothes and catch up with some decorating.)

Thanks to Jo Christian and all the team at Pimpernel Press for the encouragement and belief that I could actually write a sentence, let alone a whole book, and thanks too to Sarah Pyke, whose work in designing the book is beautiful.

Thanks to everyone who swapped or gave me plants, seeds, pots, tools, and garden furniture or simply good advice. I am an amateur gardener with no training at all, and I couldn't have made this garden without their help and support. In no particular order, I am grateful to Lou Bonham for the seeds, Tim and Emma for the tables

and containers, Julian Brazil for the daisies, Steven Tucker for the hazel, David Anslow for the willow sticks, my sister Jane for seedlings, Sally Ann for more seeds, Tracy Durdey and Eileen Proctor for plants and Tim Blyth for the ancient lawn edger. Thanks too to Michael Tucker for his helpfulness and bottomless toolkit. And of course to my mum and dad for the many plants and seedlings over the years, but more importantly for passing on the passion that I have for gardening. Without that, this book wouldn't even exist!

Special gardening thanks go to Beth Tarling of Seaview Cottage in Cornwall. Over the years I have spent many hours photographing her garden (and her house) for various publications, and her knowledge and enthusiasm have been very important to me. She's a brilliant gardener, with an amazing eye, and I am always happy to drop everything if she 'suggests' that something might be worth photographing.

Thank you also to the gardeners whose places I have photographed for this book: Mike Werkmeister, Tom Coward, Karen Burgess, Annie Stanford, Jan Basford, Julie Quinn, David Gordon, Helen Grimes, Piers Newth and Louise Allen, Louisa Morgan, Julia Thyer, Matt Robinson and Louise Mcclary, Louise and Fergus Dowding, Vanessa Berridge, and Fergus Garrett.

Traditionally, a village would have included, along with the church and the pub, a collection of cottages, each with its own 'cottage garden', and it has been a wonderful process trying to re-create a little bit of that. So, thanks to all the people of this village too; East Prawle is, in its way, an old-fashioned place with a tight community, and it has been a great place to build a home and garden. And in the midst of winter when it's dark by four o'clock, even though we don't have a church in the village, our local pub, The Pig's Nose Inn, just around the corner, is a beacon of light that keeps us all going!

INDEX